John Newton Stearns

Merry's Book of Travel and Adventure

John Newton Stearns

**Merry's Book of Travel and Adventure**

ISBN/EAN: 9783743324442

Manufactured in Europe, USA, Canada, Australia, Japa

Cover: Foto ©Andreas Hilbeck / pixelio.de

Manufactured and distributed by brebook publishing software (www.brebook.com)

John Newton Stearns

**Merry's Book of Travel and Adventure**

# MERRY'S BOOK

## OF

# TRAVEL AND ADVENTURE.

EDITED BY
UNCLE MERRY.

NEW-YORK:
H. DAYTON, No. 36 HOWARD STREET.
INDIANAPOLIS, IND.: ASHER & CO.
1860.

# CONTENTS.

| | PAGE |
|---|---|
| Adventures at Sea, | 13 |
| About Valleys, Plains and Deserts, | 19 |
| Giotto, the Shepherd Boy and Painter, | 36 |
| The Artist, | 43 |
| Thrilling Adventure, | 50 |
| Winnipiseogee and the Legend of Chocorua, | 56 |
| A Fearful Adventure—Almost, | 61 |
| The Alpine Herd Boy, | 66 |
| A Conversation About Islands, | 76 |
| The Man with the Iron Mask, | 89 |
| Travels about Africa, | 99 |
| The Highlands of Scotland, | 108 |
| Elsie's Summer Adventures, | 125 |
| Adventure of a Dog, | 142 |
| The Gladiators, | 150 |
| The Four Henrys, | 154 |
| Spectre of the Brocken, | 159 |
| King Roderick and the Enchanted Cavern, | 167 |
| The Mountain Lute, | 172 |
| Dushmanta, | 178 |
| Gypsies, | 182 |
| Little Four-Toes, | 185 |
| The Elves of the Forest Centre, | 190 |
| Adventures of Catlin, | 195 |
| The Panther Hunt, | 198 |

## CONTENTS.

|  | PAGE |
|---|---|
| The Mammoth Cave, | 209 |
| The Pump, | 214 |
| A Banker in Trouble, | 217 |
| Ruins of St. Bartolph at Colchester, | 221 |
| My Heart's in the Highlands, | 225 |
| The Highlander's Song, | 226 |
| The Palace of the Escurial, | 229 |
| Tomb of Edward II., | 230 |
| Church of the Holy Trinity, Hull, | 233 |
| The Serpent of Rhodes, | 236 |

# ENGRAVINGS.

|                                              | PAGE         |
|----------------------------------------------|--------------|
| Frontispiece,                                | 2            |
| Northern Icebergs,                           | 12           |
| Arctic Sea,                                  | 15           |
| The Light-House,                             | 17           |
| Valleys 'mid the Mountains,                  | 19           |
| Scene Among the Mountains,                   | 27           |
| The Shepherd Boy and Painter,                | 37           |
| The Artist,                                  | 42           |
| Winnipiseogee,                               | 56           |
| Residence of the Alpine Herd Boy             | 66           |
| The Alps,                                    | 70           |
| Mount Vesuvius,                              | 79           |
| A Volcanic Island,                           | 81           |
| Bolabola,                                    | 87           |
| The Captive Arriving at the Bastile,         | 92           |
| African Chiefs,                              | 100, 101, 103|
| Lake Scenery,                                | 109          |
| High Mountain,                               | 111          |
| The Highlanders,                             | 112          |
| Loch Katrine,                                | 113          |
| Loch Awe,                                    | 121          |
| Isle of Staffa,                              | 123          |
| The Sailing Party,                           | 125          |
| Diamond Cove,                                | 132          |
| Parley with the Indians,                     | 134          |
| The Safe Return,                             | 139          |

|  | PAGE |
|---|---|
| "Jerry," | 142 |
| The Gladiators, | 150 |
| Spectre of the Brocken, | 161 |
| Mont Blanc, | 172 |
| The Lute Player, | 175 |
| Alpine Mountains, | 177 |
| The Lost Child and the Gypsies, | 182 |
| Dance of the Fairies, | 191 |
| The Hound, | 199 |
| The Mammouth Cave, | 208 |
| The Pump, | 215 |
| Ruins at St. Bartolph at Colchester, | 222 |
| My Heart's in the Highlands, | 225 |
| Tomb of Edward II., | 231 |
| Church of the Holy Trinity, Hull, | 233 |
| The Knight's Farewoll, | 238 |

# PREFACE.

THE world we live on is not a very large one. It is very small compared with the sun, or even with Jupiter. And in the great universe of God, it is a mere speck. And yet how small a part of it do any of us ever see! How little do we know about any part of the world, except the little neighborhood or State where we chance to reside. Some few men have traveled over a considerable portion of the earth. But few, even of those called travelers, have seen more than here and there a spot of the four great quarters of the earth. Those of us who cannot travel abroad are much indebted to those who can, for writing accounts of their travels, of the countries they have passed through, the people they have seen, the adventures they have met with. We have, in some sort, the advantage of going along with them, when we read their books. We see with their eyes, and hear with their ears, and so become acquainted with the distant places and people genii and ghosts, which the imagination of man could invent. These amuse for a time, just while we are reading them; but there is nothing left to remember or think of when the reading is finished. The tales and stories of this volume are such that you can tell the tales as often as you please, without being called *a telltale;* and the stories without being set down as a *storyteller.*

To enjoy a tale or a story, it should be read aloud among a little circle of friends. It should be read well, so that every one can hear and understand it. The great fault in reading stories, is, that they are read too rapidly, as if the only aim were to get as soon as possible to the end. This is one reason why novel reading is so injurious. It is skimmed over, and rushed through, at railroad speed, so that nothing is thought of, as you go along, and nothing remembered after you get through, but just the outline of the story. The moral is entirely disregarded, and the fine sentiments that may be expressed by any of the characters, or the beautiful sentences they may chance to have uttered, are all lost, and a careless habit of reading without reflection is formed.

As a matter of course, such reading is bad in other respects. Very rapid reading can never be good reading. It can never give good emphasis and expression to the words, and can never assist the reader to a good style of education. Many a good speaker has been spoiled by cultivating a bad habit of reading. Such a habit of reading also greatly injures and weakens the memory. For, we are so much the creatures of habit, and bad habits are so much more early formed, and so much more difficult to shake off than good ones, that this same habit of careless, unreflecting reading will be sure to follow us and stick to us. We shall read other books hastily and carelessly, and of course shall not remember what we read. And the attention, not being always chained to what we read, will learn to wander, so that we cannot control it when we wish to. And the memory, not duly exercised and stored with valuable treasures, will become indolent, and weak, and unreliable. The loss sustained by a young person, in forming such a careless habit of reading, cannot be made up. No after effort will recover it.

We trust our young friends will all remember this, and never allow themselves to read, without close attention and fixed thought, and a sturdy purpose to treasure up for future use everything that is of sufficient value to make it worth while to read it at all.

# Book of Travel and Adventure.

## ADVENTURES AT SEA.

THERE are some adventures in the history of every sailor, that are not only worth relating, but worth all the trouble, pain, and weariness they cost. Let me very briefly, touch on a few of my own.

We were in a very high latitude, and on the lookout for ice. One morning, at daybreak, we found ourselves in the neighborhood of several immense icebergs, and surrounded, on every side, with floating ice. It was a scene of great sublimity and beauty. Here were some forty or fifty floating mountains, or islands, with mountain cones shooting up over all their surface, and reaching to the height of from 300 to 500 feet. They were of dif-

ferent dimensions, and heights, and presented a great variety of aspects. Sometimes they would glisten and blaze in the light of the sun, like cliffs of pure crystal. Sometimes one of the huge cliffs would throw its dark shadow upon the other, and change the dazzling glow to a cold, bleak, inhospitable frown. Occasionally, as portions of the surface melted in the sunbeams, or as the spray dashed up the sides of the cliff, little rills would be formed, and rushing together into one, dash down furiously to the depths below. We came to anchor under the lee of one of those ice-mountains, and sent out our boats to reconnoitre for an outlet. The men, well attired and otherwise prepared for the work, disembarked on the ice, clambered up the rugged and slippery cliffs, with the aid of spears.

# TRAVEL AND ADVENTURE. 15

THE ARCTIC SEA.

harpoons, and boat-hooks, and seemed greatly to enjoy the sport. On one of the cliffs, they found a polar bear who had deserted his Arctic home, and taken free passage for a warmer clime. They tried to capture him, but he was too wide awake for that, so they left him to his fate, which was probably a grave in the Gulf-stream.

After a long succession of calms and adverse winds, which seemed to combine against us, we came, at length, in sight of land. It was a dark, lowering night. The storm was just passing away, but the waves were rolling and dashing with great fury. A little after midnight, the man at the bow cried out, "land-ho!—a light!" All hands were soon on deck, eager to catch the first glimpse of home, and taste the fresh breeze from land. As the ship rose and fell on the billows, the distant light was seen at intervals, and then lost to view. We were making directly towards it, with the wind in our favor. As we advanced, the bright beacon before us loomed higher and higher into the sky, and shed, far away on the crests of the broken waves, a strong glare of light. The clouds began to scud and break, and the moon from behind them gave us occasional glimpses of the rock-bound coast. Far away to leeward, a ship was noticed, under close-reefed topsails, laboring in the swollen sea, and evidently suffering from the effects of the storm. The dashing of the waves against the crag-

gy coast, kept up a tremendous roar, as of distant thunder. And when, occasionally, a wave heavier than the rest, concentrating the force of a dozen in one, dashed up against the base of the beacon, it would break, and rise in spray and foam, almost to its very top, and then scatter on every side, in a deluge of baffled fury. Over all this, the steady light, unmoved from its firm foundations, continued to shine, and to guide us on our homeward way. To those, who have traversed the ocean, or escaped a tempest, the incident may seem trifling. But no one who has experienced the full force of the word "home," and rest, after such a scene, will fail to sympathize with the feeling that invests the light-house near home with a character bordering on the sacred. Many a sailor would write "Home, sweet home," on its corner stone.

## ABOUT VALLEYS, PLAINS, AND DESERTS.

PERHAPS our readers have nearly forgotten the conversation which Mary, Henry, and Robert had with their father while on their way to Staten Island. The children were then talking about islands. They are very inquisitive, and whenever they can find their father at leisure they are sure to gather around him with a thousand questions about whatever subject may have engaged their attention. In this way their lessons at school and and the books that they read at home, all come up for discussion, and they have a great many pleasant evenings together. Mary says it is a thousand times pleasanter than the children's parties which she sometimes attends, and Robert says he had rather stay at home when his father is at leisure than to go to the Crystal Palace.

We happened in last evening, just as they had got seated cozily together, and Mary was saying,

"Papa, what shall we talk about to-night? Last night it was all about mountains, snowy mountains, and burning mountains—I don't believe we can find any other subject so interesting."

"To-night, we will talk about valleys," said her papa.

Henry looked disappointed on hearing this; for he thought there could be nothing very remarkable about valleys.

"Our village lies in a valley," said he, "and it is a pretty one, with plenty of trees and a river; but I do not see anything particular in it. What can you be going to tell us about valleys, papa?"

"I am going to tell you about the valleys which lie among lofty mountains, and you will soon find that they are altogether different from our own little valley."

"They are a great deal larger, I suppose," said Mary.

"They are usually much deeper," replied her father, "lying between the opposite ridges of mountains, and often appearing very much like a cleft, or mere splitting open of the mountains."

"Do you think the mountains did ever split open, papa?" asked Robert.

"In some cases there is every reason to believe that they did. In the two great mountain chains of Europe, the Alps and the Pyrenees, the sides of some of the valleys so exactly correspond with each other, that, if it were possible to force them together, they would fit into each other quite closely, and scarcely a trace of any opening would remain."

"I suppose there must have been some great earthquakes, to split open the mountains in that way," remarked Henry.

"As you learn more about the structure of the earth," said his father, "you will find that many wonderful changes appear to have passed upon it since the creation. For some purposes unknown to us, it has pleased God at some period to 'shake terribly the earth,' so that vast numbers of the lower animals have been buried in its ruins. The remains of these are frequently dug out of the earth, and are called *fossils*. The whole subject is full of wonders, and is too difficult for you at present;

but when we come to a fact like this splitting asunder of mighty mountains, we may well lift our thoughts to that Being who 'looketh on the earth, and it trembleth ; who toucheth the hills, and they smoke.' Ps. civ. 32."

" I should be almost afraid to live among mountains," said Mary. " I dare say they are very beautiful, but they seem to be dangerous too. And those mountain valleys must be gloomy sort of places."

" The entrances to some of the higher valleys are exceedingly narrow and gloomy," said her father. " They are very narrow openings, called *passes* or *defiles*. They are called passes, because they form the road by which we can pass from one valley to another ; but they are sometimes so long, narrow, and winding, that they better deserve the name of *defile*, which means drawn out like a thread."

" How very different the mountain valleys are from ours !" remarked Henry. We have no splitting open of hills, no gloomy passes, nor winding defiles."

" You may well say they are different," replied his father. " A mountain valley frequently has a rapid torrent rushing through it ; or, if it be situated among snowy mountains, where the cold is severe, it forms the bed of a still more remarkable stream. I mean the *glacier*."

" Dear papa, I am glad you are going to explain what a glacier is," cried Robert.

"You will, perhaps, get some idea of its nature if I call it a river of ice," said his father. "Just as the lower valleys frequently form the beds of mountain streams, so these upper valleys become the channels of the mountain snows, which melt and freeze by turns as they descend, and so form the glacier."

"But does the snow come down from the mountain?" asked Henry. "I thought that the tops of the loftiest mountains were always covered with it, winter and summer."

"So they are," replied his father. "At a certain height the cold is so great that the vapors of the atmosphere are constantly converted into snow; therefore it is perpetual snow above that height, but not below it. The point at which this change takes place is called the *snow line*. Below that line the snow soon gives way, and becomes a peculiar sort of ice, filling the valleys and forming glaciers."

"But why do you call the glacier a *river* of ice, papa? A river is always flowing, but ice cannot flow."

"If it can not flow, it can move; and this the whole glacier does at a slow and silent pace."

"Can people see it move as they look down into the valley?" asked Mary.

"No, they cannot see it move, nor can they feel it when they are walking on the glacier."

Henry was astonished to find that any one could walk on a glacier; and he found it difficult to understand what sort of ice it could be which would move onwards like a river, and yet be firm enough to allow of people walking upon it. Robert wanted to know how any one could be sure that the glacier moved at all, if he could neither see it move nor feel it.

His papa told him that there was no difficulty about that, for by fixing a rod firmly in the ice of the glacier, and then marking the rocky sides of the valley opposite to it, it was quite clear, that if the ice moved forward it would carry the rod with it, and so it would be seen, by the distance of the rod from the markings, how far it had traveled in a certain time. "This sort of observation was made for nearly a whole year," said he, "and it was found that the glacier-ice had moved about four hundred and eighty-one feet in that time."

"Surely, papa, it must be very dangerous to go upon this moving ice?" said Mary.

"You must ask Uncle Charles about that," replied her father. "He has traversed the glaciers from sunrise to sunset, and he will tell you of fatigues and dangers, but not from the movement of the glacier, which is quite imperceptible."

"Perhaps he was afraid the ice would break and let him sink in," said Robert.

"And suppose he were to fall in?" said Mary.

"He would then probably lose his life," replied her father, "for these crevasses are many of them of great depth."

Robert here requested to know where the glaciers go to at last, after moving along so quietly.

"They gradually descend into the lower and warmer regions, where they are greatly wasted by evaporation and melting, and where they terminate. The melted ice of glaciers runs into the crevasses, or filters through the mass, furnishing the source of considerable streams, which rush forth from icy caverns beneath the glacier. Some glaciers at their termination are several hundred feet high, and a mile across: and you may fancy that it must require considerable heat to make any impression on such a vast mass of ice."

"It must indeed, papa. And what a splendid sight this icy river must be! If it were all smooth ice instead of rough, it would make a capital skating place. Would it not be pleasant to go to the top of a glacier and skate down?"

"You must know that a glacier is sometimes twenty miles long," replied his father. "Therefore, supposing we could get rid of the gaping crevasses, and could be sure that no rocks would fall on us, and supposing also that the ice were fit to skate upon, it would still be an arduous task to accomplish."

Henry had new cause for wonder when he heard

of the great extent of the glaciers; and he began to think that they were quite as surprising and unaccountable as the volcanoes had appeared to him.

"Before we leave the mountain valleys," said his father, "I must mention the terrible devastation committed by *avalanches*."

"Oh, I have read about avalanches," said Mary, "in a story of the dogs of St. Bernard."

"And so have I," said Henry. "Avalanches are great heaps of ice and snow, that fall down suddenly from the mountains, and sometimes bury people under them."

"But why do the people walk just under the mountain?" said Mary. "I am sure if I was there, I would keep as far away from them as possible."

"In mountainous countries," replied her father, "it is impossible to travel any distance without getting into dangerous situations. Sometimes the only road from one place to another is a mere ledge on the side of the mountain."

"But is there no notice of its coming?" said Robert.

"None whatever. In an instant, and without any warning, whole tons of ice and snow, that have been long accumulated on the upper slopes of the mountain, will suddenly give way, and sweeping down with immense force, will carry before them

# TRAVEL AND ADVENTURE. 27

not only a few poor travelers, if such happen to come in their way, but also entire forests and villages."

"The avalanche causes such a tremendous rush of air, that it acts as a perfect hurricane, tearing up trees, overturning houses, and lifting masses of rock from their places."

"I am glad we are not mountaineers," said Mary. "We have storms here sometimes, but they are nothing like those avalanche winds."

"The worst storm I ever remember," said Henry, "was when the old elm was blown down, and when nearly all the glass in the greenhouse was broken. That was a terrible storm, but it must be like a gentle breeze compared with those winds that lift up rocks and overturn houses."

"True," replied his father; "and no doubt a pious mountaineer, feeling the dangerous circumstances in which he is placed, must have a most simple and perfect trust in God, or he could not enjoy that peace and contentment which he is often found to possess. Travelers tell us that the language of the mountain guides is often highly expressive of faith and dependence, and would do honor to better educated Christians."

"I am very glad they are good people," said Mary, "because God will take care of them in their mountain homes."

Henry now inquired whether there were any

dangers in those lower valleys, which his father had described as the beds of rapid rivers; and he was told that the chief danger arises from the streams becoming greatly increased by some unusual melting of the snows in the upper valleys. "When this is the case," he added, "the torrent becomes exceedingly rapid and impetuous, so that in entering wider valleys it bursts from its usual course, and overspreads the country to a great extent, causing ruinous floods, to the destruction of life and property."

The children began to ask whether their own little valley might not, at some time or other, be flooded by the swelling of the river; and when they found that such an event was not impossible, they were puzzled to decide what sort of places are really safe to live in. "Mountains are not very safe," said Mary, "and valleys are not very safe, and what other places are there where we could be out of danger?"

"O, I know!" cried Robert; "the plain is a safe place to live in, we should never meet with glaciers, or avalanches, or volcanoes there."

"But what is the rest of the world to do?" said Mary.

"I dare say there are plains enough in all parts of the world."

"*Plains*, my boy," said his father, "form the greatest part of the earth's surface. Some plains are raised many thousand feet above the sea, and others, on the contrary, are in very low situations, and appear to have been once covered by the ocean. The most elevated plains lie among mountains, and are called table-lands. They are principally found in Asia and America, the plains of Europe being of a middle height."

Henry said he did not expect to hear of plains among mountains, and he could not think why they should be called table-lands.

"Simply because they have a level surface like a table, and are higher than the plains around them. Properly speaking, those only are table-lands which are raised abruptly from the surrounding country, to the height of many hundred feet above the level of the sea. The lofty plains of Quito, in South America, are twelve thousand feet above the sea; and the table-lands of Mexico, in North America, are from five to ten thousand feet above the sea level."

"What fine large tables!" cried Mary. "I hope they are well covered with provisions."

"Quite the reverse," said her father. "Only a few hardy kinds of grass grow on these table-lands, affording but very poor pasturage. Rain falls in abundance from April to July, but it does not enrich this barren soil, which consists of sand mixed with chalk."

"I suppose the low plains are not so badly off," said Henry.

"Some of them are extremely rich and fertile, as the plain of Lombardy, which is covered with villages and towns, and has been cultivated with so much success that, when seen from the Alps, it looks like an immense garden. There are many other plains in Europe, America, and Africa. According to their situation and character they are known by different names ; the immense plains in the central parts of North America are called *Savannas* or *Prairies ;* they are generally very fertile and are covered with great quantities of tall rank grass. When the grass becomes dried it sometimes takes fire accidentally ; at other times it is set on fire by the Indians. This fire does little damage where the plains are elevated and the grass is short, but when the tall heavy grass of the lower plains is burning, it forms an awful sight, and sometimes occasions loss of life."

" How is that, papa ?" said Robert ; "cannot people get out of the way of it ?"

" When once a prairie is on fire, there is no stopping the flames, and they are carried onward according to the direction and violence of the wind ; therefore, persons traveling in these vast solitudes may be overtaken by such a fire, and find the greatest difficulty in escaping."

" But if they are on horseback, they can surely ride faster than the fire can travel," said Henry.

" They might do so in any other situation, but the

tall grass, which is often festooned with creeping plants, entangles their horses' feet, and makes it necessary that they should keep in the track of the deer or buffalo, which is often a zigzag and not a direct path."

"Do the deer and buffalo run away from the fire too?" asked Mary.

"Yes. We are told that all animals flee before this fiery tempest, and put forth their utmost power to reach an elevated part of the prairie, where the grass is short and the danger less extreme. These hillocks or elevations of the prairie are called *prairie-bluffs*. Such are the plains of North America. The interior of South America is also remarkable for the extent of its plains."

"I had no idea there were so many great plains in the world," said Henry; "I never heard even their names, for they are not marked on the map."

"Perhaps you have never heard of the great plains of Asia, called the *Steppes*, and yet they are reckoned to occupy a space of about a million square miles."

"What is a *square* mile?" said Robert.

"A piece of ground which is a mile long and a mile broad."

"And why are these great plains called Steppes?" said Henry.

"Because they are raised the one above the other like steps."

"What enormous steps!" said Mary. "Fit to match with the tables on the mountains, and the cups of the volcanoes."

"I need not attempt to describe these Steppes, or the other plains of Asia. You have now, I hope, a general notion of the nature of such plains as are either cultivated, or yield naturally some kind of vegetation; but I have yet to speak of another kind of plains, which are extremely barren, and are known as deserts. The most extensive desert in the world is the Sahara or Great Desert of Africa, which occupies a vast space in the central parts of that continent. That desert is said to be more than two-thirds the size of Europe."

"That is the place where the camel is so useful," said Mary; "he is called the ship of the desert, for no one can cross it without him. He has a sort of padded foot, that is just fit for walking on sands. There is a great deal about the desert in my history of the camel."

"Deserts are very dreary kinds of plains, are they not, papa?" said Robert; "plains that would not be pleasant to live in!"

"They are plains which it is even dangerous to cross, much more to live in," replied his father.

"The greater part of the African desert we have been speaking of is covered with moving sands, raised into ridges like waves, and continually shifting by the effect of the wind. There is, therefore, no road, or beaten track, for travelers."

"Then, how do they find their way?" said Henry.

"Chiefly by the pole-star, which is also the guide of mariners at sea. Indeed we may call the desert a sea of sand, navigated by that valuable animal, the camel, which as Mary says, is called the ship of the desert."

"And if they are able to find their way, are they safe from any other danger?"

"By no means; they may be overtaken by sand-storms, in which the simoom or hot wind sweeps over the desert with great fury, and often suffocates or buries, in drifting sand, the unfortunate traveler."

"What do travelers do while the whirlwind lasts?" asked Henry.

"They generally halt in their journey, protect their faces as well as they can, and kneel or lie down near their camels."

"But what do they do for food while passing those dreary wastes?"

"They carry enough to last them till they reach one of those spots of which there are a few in the desert, where water is to be found. Such a spot is called an *oasis*, and presents a patch of verdure, and perhaps a few shrubs and flowers, growing around the fountain or well. To the traveler who has been long on the desert it is a little paradise, and he describes it in the most enthusiastic terms; but much of its beauty in his eyes is derived, no doubt, from the contrast with the sandy wastes he has been traversing."

"It must be very pleasant to them to walk upon the grass once more, after being so long upon the hot dry sand," said Henry; "and to have plenty of spring water, instead of a small allowance from their bottles."

"Sad is the disappointment which sometimes happens to the travelers on arriving at the wells, to find that they are dried up. They then have to travel as quickly as possible to the next place where they are likely to find water; and the poor distressed camels are as eager to reach the spot as their masters. At such times a strange appearance often cheats the eyes of those who are unaccustomed to the desert. At a short distance from them they seem to perceive lakes of water, but on approaching nearer they entirely vanish. This appearance is owing to the great heat of the surface of the earth, and to an effect of the sun's rays called *refraction*. The name given to these singular appearances is the *mirage*."

"How it must vex them to be deceived in that way when they are so thirsty!" said Mary.

It was now nine o'clock, and the children bid their father good-night, and retired to rest.

THE SHEPHERD-BOY AND PAINTER.

## GIOTTO, THE SHEPHERD-BOY AND PAINTER.

ABOUT forty miles from Florence, Italy, there lived a poor peasant, named Bondone. In 1276 he had a son born, whom he called Giotto. The father was an ignorant man, and knew little else than to labor in taking care of his flocks of sheep.

There were no public schools in that country, where children of the poor man, as well as those of the rich, could attend and obtain an education. Consequently, young Giotto was brought up in ignorance. But he was one of those boys that learn something from what they see around them.

In the country where Giotto lived, there were no fences and fields such as we have, to keep the sheep and cattle from straying ; hence it was necessary to keep some person with the flocks while they were feeding on the plains, to take care of them.

At the early age of ten, Bondone sent his son Giotto out to take care of a flock. This pleased the lad, for now the happy little shepherd-boy could roam about the meadow plain at his will. But most of his time must be spent near the flock, and he was not long in devising some means to keep himself busy while there.

His favorite amusement soon became that of sketching in the sand, or on broad flat stones, making pictures of surrounding objects, while lying on the grass, in the midst of his flock. His pencils were a hard stick or a sharp piece of stone, and his chief models the sheep which gathered around him in various attitudes.

The following story is related of the manner in which the genius of Giotto was discovered, and how he became a great painter.

One day, as the shepherd-boy lay in the midst of his flock, earnestly sketching something on a stone, there came by a traveler. Struck with the boy's deep attention to his work, and the unconscious grace of his attitude, the stranger stopped and went to look at what he was doing.

It was the sketch of a sheep, drawn with such freedom and truth to nature, that the traveler beheld it with astonishment.

"Whose son are you?" said he, with eagerness.

The startled boy looked in the face of his questioner. "My father is Bondone, the laborer, and I am his little Giotto, so please the signor," said he.

"Well, then, little Giotto, should you like to come and live with me, and learn how to draw, and paint sheep like this, and horses, and even men?"

The child's eye flashed with delight.

"I will go with you any where to learn that. But," he added, as a sudden reflection made him change color, "I must first go and ask my father; I can do nothing without his leave."

"That is right, my boy, and so we will go to him together," said the stranger, who was the painter Ciambue.

Great was the wonder of old Bondone at such a sudden proposal; but he perceived his son's wish, though Giotto was fearful of expressing it, and consented. He accompanied his boy to Florence, and left his little Giotto under the painter's care.

His pupil's progress surpassed Ciambue's expectations. In delineating nature, Giotto soon went beyond his master, to whom a good deal of the formality of the Greek art, which he had been the first to cast aside, still clung.

One morning the artist came into his studio, and looking at a half-finished head, saw a fly resting on the nose. Ciambue tried to brush it off, when he discovered that it was only painted.

"Who has done this?" cried he, half angry, half delighted.

Giotto came trembling from a corner, and confessed his fault. But he met with praise instead of reproof from his master, who loved art too well to be indignant at his pupil's talent, even though the frolic were directed against himself.

As Giotto grew older, his fame spread far and wide. Like most artists of those early times, he was an architect as well as a painter. Pope Benedict IX. sent messengers to him one day. They entered the artist's studio, and informed him that the Pope intended to employ him in designing for St. Peter's Church in Rome, and that he desired Giotto to send him some designs that he might judge of his capacity.

Giotto was a pleasant and humorous man, and, taking a sheet of paper, he drew with one stroke of his pencil a perfect circle. Then, handing it to the messengers, he said to them, "There is my design, take that to his holiness."

The messenger replied, "I ask for a design." "Go, sir," said Giotto; "I tell you his holiness asks nothing else of me." And notwithstanding all their remonstrance, he refused to give any other.

Pope Benedict was a learned man; he saw that Giotto had given the best instance of perfection in his art, sent for him to come to Rome, and honored and rewarded him. From this incident, "Round as Giotto's O," became an Italian proverb.

The talents of Giotto won him the patronage of the great of his country. He visited in succession Padua, Verona, and Ferrara. At the latter city he remained some time, painting for the Prince of Este.

While there, Dante heard of Giotto, and invited him to Ravenna. There, also, he painted many of his works, and formed a strong friendship with the great Dante.

The poor shepherd-boy was now in the height of his fame. Admitted into the society of the Italian nobles, enjoying the friendship of the talented men of his age—Dante, Boccaccio, and Petrarch—his was indeed an enviable position.

He was a good man as well as great, loved by all his friends; and, as his biographer, Vassari, says, "a good Christian as well as an excellent painter." He died at Milan in the year 1336, and the city of Florence erected a statue in honor of this great artist.

THE ARTIST.

## THE ARTIST.

WE have something to tell you about Franklin Ames, and we presume you will be glad to hear it. It relates to the state of his hands, and the discovery which he made, that mortar was not plaster. That discovery, together with his sore hands, had a dampering effect upon his zeal to become an artist. It was harder work than he thought it was. The glory to be gained seemed to recede to a greater distance. His materials for statuary turned into common stone again, the idea of modeling became decidedly unpleasant. The word Studio did not sound half as well as it did before.

Still he had within him the elements of perseverance. He did not like to give up a thing when he had once undertaken it—an excellent trait of character, which I hope the reader will labor to acquire, for it is one of the best aids to success in life.

I would not have the reader understand the above remark after the manner in which a boy in a boarding-school understands it—or rather pretended to understand it. The teacher was expatiating on the subject of perseverance. It is true that, in the course of his remarks, he spoke of the importance of choosing good ends, but the last sentence he uttered was, "be slow in forming a resolution to do a thing, but having formed it, persevere at all hazards."

A young lad sat at his desk and took notes of the advice, and wrote out in full the last sentence. The teacher was rather pleased to have so much attention paid to his remarks.

In the teacher's garden there was a very fine plum tree, small but laden with excellent fruit. Young John watched it carefully, and as soon as the plums fairly began to turn purple, he diminished the quantity. This was done at night. In the morning the teacher saw that some one had been robbing his plum tree. The wall was so high, that there was little probability that the robbery was committed by any person from without. He therefore mentioned the fact of the robbery to his boys, and appealed to their sense of justice and of honor to prevent a recurrence of the act.

But it was soon repeated. In fact, about as fast as the fruit turned purple it was stolen. At length the teacher determined to watch during the whole night. By that means he caught young John in the felonious act.

The next morning, he called him to account for his conduct before the school.

"How came you to do it?" said he to the delinquent.

"I did it in accordance with your directions, sir."

"What do you mean, you insulting boy?"

"You told us to be slow in forming a resolution to do a thing, but having formed it, to persevere at all hazards! I wrote down your words at the time, sir," taking his notes from his desk. "I was a long time forming the resolution. I began to think about it when the plum tree was in blossom, I kept thinking about it all the while the plums were growing, and never formed the resolution to take them until they began to turn. Having began to take them, I thought I must persevere, though I knew I should be caught."

"Why so?"

"Because you said we must persevere at all hazards."

"I shall pursue the same course with respect to your punishment; you may go to your chamber; when I have formed my resolution to punish you, I shall send for you, and you may rely upon it, I shall persevere in it at all hazards."

He went to his room and spent a very long day there. At sunset he was sent for to the schoolroom, and received a very persevering application of a rod to his back.

But I sat down to tell you something more about Franklin Ames. While he was in the state of mind described above, his favorite uncle came to see him. Uncle Henry was not as busy a man as his brother. He had time to attend to his children, and a fine flock of them he had. He and his boys walked and talked, and sometimes played together as if they had been companions. The boys were never more happy than when they were with their father, and everybody said they will be just like their father, and the tone in which those words were uttered, indicated, that to be like their father was a very praiseworthy and desirable thing.

Uncle Henry felt a great interest in Franklin, and when he visited the family, he always talked more with him than with any other member of the family. He had a way of drawing out of him all his plans and desires. Franklin was never afraid to tell him anything, he felt sure of his sympathy, sure that he would not laugh at him even if he thought his plans were foolish. He had not been long in the house before he had the whole history of the studio.

"What do you think of my plan of being an artist, uncle?" said Franklin.

"Well, I have not had time to think much about it," said Uncle Henry; "I will think about it. It is a great thing to be a refined artist. I should like to see you one."

"Then I will be one."

"You must take more time to consider and decide. And then there are various kinds of artists, and I don't know in what line you would be likely to succeed the best."

" I wish to be a sculptor."

" You wish to make perfect forms of men in marble ?"

" Yes, sir."

" There is a fine art much superior to that of sculpture."

" What is it ? Painting ?"

" No, it is the art of making a strong, beautiful and perfect mind. That is the art which I should like to have you learn first ; great artists in this line take rank before all others."

" I never heard of any such."

" Did you ever hear of one George Washington ?"

" Yes, sir, I am rather inclined to think I have."

" What is his reputation ?"

" It is a little ahead of that of any man who has lived."

" And what is it owing to ?"

" His actions."

" And what did his actions spring from ?"

" From his principles."

" And where did he get his principles ?"

Franklin could not answer the last question as promptly as he had answered those which preceded it. He was in doubt whether to say they were born with him, or whether he had formed them himself, and after a little farther reflection, he thought the truth lay between the two.

" Washington's actions," said Uncle Henry, "were

simply the exponents of his mind. If he had not had a powerful, wise, just, and noble mind, could he have performed the actions which have given him his renown?"

"No, sir."

"Certainly not. Washington prepared himself for his sublime career by the most careful culture of the mind, and it was owing to the fact that he became a most consummate artist in respect to the culture of mind, and the formation of character, that he was enabled to perform his matchless deeds in the field and in the cabinet."

"Washington did not bestow much care on the cultivation of his mind. He did not go to school much, and he never went near a college."

"I must be allowed to differ from you, my boy, on that point. Washington did bestow the utmost care on the cultivation of his mind."

"He never studied Latin or Greek, and he could not have studied many books; for there were not many books within his reach."

"It is true that he had not the advantages of instruction which are now within the reach of almost every boy in the country, but nevertheless he succeeded in forming the most perfect human mind of which we have any knowledge."

"He did not create his own talents."

"No, his talents—the elements of his character—were given him by Providence, but the formation of that character, which has been and still is the admiration of the world, was his own work. He did not let his mind run to waste. He did not let the form of his character be determined by circumstances. He did not throw the responsibility of his improvement on his teachers. He pursued a course similar to that of the sculptor who wishes to produce a most perfect specimen of art. The sculptor first forms a conception of the thing he wishes to make, the end which he desires to attain, and then bends all his energies with untiring industry to the realization of that conception, the attainment of that end. So with Washington. He formed the conception of a pure, lofty, symmetrical character, and took unwearied pains to realize it, and he succeeded."

"Do you think any one else could do the same thing?"

"I do not suppose any one could acquire his reputation; for the reputation of men depends in part upon the circumstances in which they are placed. I will say this: if any one will take as much pains in the cultivation of his mind and the formation of his character as Washington took, he will have a noble character and will stand high in the estimation of his fellow men. Let it be your first object of ambition to become an artist in the sense I have now explained the term."

## THRILLING ADVENTURE.

FATHER will have done the great chimney to-night, won't he, mother? said little Tommy Howard, as he stood waiting for his father's breakfast, which he carried to him at his work every morning.

"He said he hoped that all the scaffolding would be down to-night," answered the mother, "and that'll be a fine night, for I never like the ending of those great chimneys; it is so risky for father to be last up."

"Oh, then, but I'll go and see him, and help 'em to give a shout before he comes down." said Tom.

"And then," continued the mother, "if all goes on right, we are to have a frolic to-morrow, and go into the country, and take our dinner, and spend all the day long in the woods."

"Hurrah!" cried Tom, as he ran off to his father's place of work, with a can of milk in one hand, and some bread in the other. His mother stood at the door, watching him, as he went merrily whistling down the street, and she thought of the dear father he was going to, and the dangerous work he was engaged in ; and then her heart sought its sure refuge, and she prayed to God to protect and bless her treasures.

Tom, with a light heart, pursued his way to his father, and leaving him his breakfast, went to his own work, which was at some distance. In the evening, on his way home, he went round to see how his father was getting along.

James Howard, the father, and a number of other workmen, had been building one of those lofty chimneys which, in manufacturing towns, almost supply the place of other architectural beauty. The chimney was of the highest and most tapering that had ever been erected, and as Tom shaded his eyes from the slanting rays of the setting sun, and looked in search of his father, his heart sank within him at the appalling sight. The scaffold was almost down, the men at the bottom were removing the beams and poles. Tom's father stood alone at the top.

He then looked around to see that all was right, and then waving his hat in the air, the men below answered him with a long, loud cheer, little Tom shouting as loud as any of them. As their voices died away, however, they heard a different sound, a cry of horror and alarm from above. The men looked around, and coiled upon the ground lay the rope, which, before the scaffolding was removed, should have been fastened to the chimney, for Tom's father to come down by. The scaffolding had been taken down without remembering to take the rope up. There was a dead silence. They all knew it was impossible to throw the rope up high enough to reach the top of the chimney, or even if possible, it would hardly be safe. They stood in silent dismay, unable to give any help, or think of any means of safety.

And Tom's father, he walked round and round the little circle, the dizzy height seeming more and more fearful, and the solid earth further and further from him. In the sudden panic he lost his presence of mind, his senses failed him. He shut his eyes; he felt as if the next moment he must be dashed to pieces on the ground below.

The day passed as industriously as usual with Tom's mother at home. She was always busily employed for her husband or children in some way or other, and to-day she had been harder at work than usual getting ready for the holiday to-morrow. She had just finished her arrangements, and her thoughts were silently thanking God for the happy home, and for all those blessings, when Tom ran in.

His face was white as ashes, and he could hardly get the words out, "Mother! mother! he cannot get down!"

"Who lad—thy father?" asked the mother.

"They have forgotten to leave him the rope," answered Tom, still scarcely able to speak. His mother started up, horror struck, and stood for a moment as if paralyzed, and then pressing her hands over her face, as if to shut out the terrible picture, and breathing a prayer to God for help, she rushed out of the house.

When she reached the place where her husband was at work, a crowd gathered around the foot of the chimney, and stood quite helpless, gazing up with faces full of sorrow.

"He says he'll throw himself down."

"Thee munna do that, lad," cried the wife, with a clear, hopeful voice; "thee munna do that—wait a bit. Take off the stocking, lad, and unravel it, and let down the thread with a bit of mortar. Dost thou hear me, Jem?"

The man made a sign of assent, for it seemed as if he could not speak—and taking off his stockings unraveled the worsted yarn, row after row. The people stood around in breathless silence and suspense, wondering what Tom's mother could be thinking of, and why she sent him away in such haste for the carpenter's ball of twine.

"Let down one end of the thread with a bit of stone, and keep fast hold of the other," cried she to her husband. The little thread came waving down the tall chimney, blown hither and thither by the wind, but it reached the outstretched hands that were waiting it. Tom held the ball of twine, whilst his mother tied one end of it to the thread.

"Now, pull it slowly," cried she to her husband, and she gradually unwound the string until it reached her husband. "Now, hold the string fast, and pull," cried she, and the string grew heavy and hard to pull, for Tom and his mother had fastened a thick rope to it. They watched it gradually and slowly uncoiling from the ground, and the string was drawn higher.

There was but one coil left. It had reached the top. "Thank God!" exclaimed the wife. She hid her face in her hands in silent prayer, and rejoiced. The iron to which it should be fastened was there all right—but would her husband be able to make use of it? Would not the terror of the past have so unnerved him as to prevent him from taking the necessary measures for safety? She did not know the magical influence which her few words had exercised over him. She did not know the strength that the sound of her voice, so calm and steadfast, had filled him—as if the little thread that carried to him the hope of life once more, had conveyed to him some portion of that faith in God, which nothing ever destroyed or shook in her pure heart. She did not know that as she waited there, the words came over him, "Why art thou cast down. O, my soul, why art thou disquieted within me? hope thou in God." She lifted her heart to God for hope and strength, but could do nothing more for her husband, and her heart turned to God and rested on him as on a rock.

There was a great shout. "He's safe, mother, he's safe!" cried Tom.

"Thou hast saved my life, my Mary," said her husband, folding her in his arms.

"But what ails you? you seem more sorry than glad about it." But Mary could not speak, and if the strong arm of her husband had not held her up she would have fallen to the ground—the sudden joy after such fear had overcome her.

"Tom, let thy mother lean on thy shoulder," said his father, "and we will take her home." And in their happy home they poured forth thanks to God for his great goodness, and their happy life together felt dearer and holier for the peril it had been in, and the nearness of the danger had brought them unto God. And the holiday next day—was it not indeed a thanksgiving day?

## WINNIPISEOGEE AND THE LEGEND OF CHOCORUA.

How many boys and girls in reciting a Geography lesson upon the state of New Hampshire have hesitated and stammered in vain attempts to pronounce the long word Winnipiseogee, which is said to be " a beautiful body of water, surrounded by a country abounding in romantic scenery."

True, it is a hard word, and truer still is the description following. A few days ago a class of little girls were reciting to me this very sentence; and when I told them that the strange formidable looking word should be pronounced " Win-ne-pe-saw-ge," they opened their eyes very wide ; and as I went on to speak of the enchanting beauty of that clear lake embosomed in the hills, with its hundreds of green islands scattered over it as if a shower of emeralds had fallen there ; of the gray old mountain sentinels which rear their tall heads so thickly around, keeping guard as it were, over a scene too beautiful for mortal eye to rest on, their eyes opened wider and sparkled brighter ; and then when I told them that the name by which the rude Indians christened this lonely lake means " the smile of the Great Spirit," their interested countenances were lighted up as if they had caught some of its glory.

And I assure you, children, that often as I have glided over these clear waters in the fairy-like boat which all the summer long dances in and out among the green islands, and watched the varied charms of the scenery round, I have felt that the " smile " still lingered there in undiminished radiance, and sweetly has it stolen into my heart and left such images of beauty as will never fade.

This lake is thirty miles in length, but our impressions of its size when passing over it are very incorrect, so thickly is it studded with islands. These are three hundred and sixty-five in number; and an old tradition says that on each return of the leap-year one more starts up from its hiding-place, and with its close sinks back again beneath the bright waters. For the truth of this, the frolicking elves that haunt these fairy-like abodes may answer, for I cannot. Some of these islands are very fertile, and contain several acres of land with fine farms and picturesque little farm-houses. Others are wild and thickly wooded, so that even the bald-eagle finds a safe retreat among the branches of the tall pines which cast their shadows in the limpid water and meet those of other islets near.

I have spoken of the mountains which surround the lake. Some of them are of considerable height. There is Whiteface Mountain, a rugged and bare looking eminence, taking its name from the appearance which is given it by a kind of white rock scattered over its side. In another direction Gunstock Mountains, and nearer Copplecrown, from the summit of which a fine view is obtained, and Red Hill, still more celebrated, with its three gracefully curving peaks, the highest being an elevation of 2,500 feet. Parties on horseback are daily seen during the summer months winding up the narrow path which leads to it, and as they pass along, each opening in the trees reveals some new charm in the scene below.

They never forget to call on "Mother Cook," a strange, gipsy-like old woman, who resides in a little hovel near the pathway, and will always entertain her guests with goat's milk and blueberries, and tell their fortunes too. This art she must have learned from the mountain spirits with whom she has long been familiar, for forty years have passed since she descended from her elevated position as "The Old Woman of the Mountain."

But the view from the top is most surpassingly beautiful. Spread out beneath your eye is the entire lake, with its less noted and smaller, but still charming sister unworthily called "Squam." The Indians must have expended their taste upon Winnipiseogee. You are encircled by a glorious amphitheatre of hills, and in the distance the eye catches the faint outlines of the White Mountains. The Indians who formerly inhabited this region called them the "Crystal Hills," and supposed their snow-capped summits to be covered with glittering silver. Here too they thought the Great Spirit resided in mountain majesty, while the beauty of his "smile" fell softly down and rested upon their own sparkling waters. To them that distant shining land was holy ground, and no Indian dared approach it.

It has been said by travelers that no scenery in Scotland or Switzerland, which hundreds cross the ocean to gaze upon, surpasses in beauty this lonely panorama which the eye feasts upon from Red Hill.

Northwest of this is a singularly shaped mountain, whose barren sides and sharp peak distinguish it from all others. This is called Chocorua Peak, and with it is connected an old Indian legend, which I will tell you.

In the early days of the American colonies, when the white man first wandered up to the hills of New Hampshire, there dwelt near this mountain a lone settler with his family. Near him lived a friendly Indian called "Chocorua," who had been in the habit of granting him many favors. One day when the white man returned from hunting, he found his house destroyed and his wife and children murdered. His suspicion fell upon the kind old Indian, and in the fury of his rage and anguish he accused him of the horrid deed, and then to revenge himself burned his hut to the ground.

Poor Chocorua, stung to madness by the cruel distrust of the white man, fled from the smoking ruins of his home, climbed to the highest peak of the mountain near, and lifting his hands wildly in the air, pronounced a curse upon the white man, his children and his lands, his corn and his cattle forever, and then with an agonizing yell, threw himself down the precipice.

From that time, it is said, the peak where the awful curse was uttered has been called Chocorua peak, and the vegetation round has never flourished, while the soil remains barren and uncultivated to the present day.

## A FEARFUL ADVENTURE—ALMOST.

CALABRIA, a province in Italy, has been celebrated, in times past, as our readers may know, on account of being the residence of fierce parties of brigands, who have without mercy waylaid and plundered many an unwary traveler. The following letter of Paul Louis Courier, a French author of some note, detailing one of his adventures in Calabria, many years ago, reminds us in some of its features, of an adventure of Audubon, the great American ornithologist, in one of his hunting excursions at the West; but the real ground of alarm in the two cases was quite different.

"I was one day traveling in Calabria. It is a country of wicked people, who, I believe, have no great liking to anybody, and are particularly illdisposed towards the French. To tell you why would be a long affair. It is enough that they hate us to death, and that the unhappy being who should chance to fall into their hands would not pass his time in the most agreeable manner. I had for my companion a fine young fellow. I do not say this to interest you—but because it is truth. In these mountains the roads are precipices, and our horses got on with the greatest difficulty. My comrade going first, a track, which appeared to him more practicable and shorter than the regular path, led us astray. It was my fault. Ought I to have trusted to a head of twenty years? We sought our way out of the woods while it was yet light; but the more we looked for the path the farther we were off it. It was a very black night, when we came close upon a very black house. We went in, and not without suspicion. But what was to be done? There we found a whole family of charcoal burners at table. At the first word they invited us to join them. My young man did not stop for much ceremony. In a minute or two we were eating and drinking in right earnest—he at least: for my own part I could not help glancing about at the place and the people. Our hosts, indeed, looked like charcoal burners; but the house! you would have taken it for an arsenal. There was nothing to be seen but muskets, pistols, sabres, knives, cutlasses. Everything displeased me, and I saw that I was in no favor myself. My comrade, on the contrary, was soon one of the family. He laughed, he chatted with them; and with an imprudence which I ought to have prevented, he at once said where we came from, where we were going, that we were Frenchmen. Think of our situation. Here we were amongst our mortal enemies, alone, benighted, far from all human aid. That nothing might be omitted that could tend to destroy us, he must play the rich man forsooth, promising these folks to pay them well for hospitality; and then he must prate about his portmanteau, earnestly beseeching them to take great care of it, and put it at the head of his bed, for he wanted no other pillow. Ah, youth, youth, how you are to be pitied! Cousin, they might have thought we carried the diamonds of the crown: the treasure in his portmanteau which gave him such anxiety consisted of the letters of his mistress.

"Supper ended, they left us. Our hosts slept below; we on the story where we had been eating. On a sort of platform raised seven or eight feet, where we were to mount by a ladder, was the bed that awaited us—a nest into which we had to introduce ourselves, by jumping over barrels filled with provisions for all the year. My comrade seized upon the bed above, and was soon fast asleep, with his head upon the precious portmanteau. I was determined to keep awake, so I made a good fire, and sat myself down. The night was almost passed over tranquilly enough, and I was beginning to be comfortable, when, just at the time when it appeared to me that day was about to break, I heard our host and his wife talking and disputing below me; and putting my ear to the

chimney which communicated with the lower room,
I perfectly distinguished these exact words of the
husband : ' *Well, well, let us see ; must we kill them
both ?*' To which the wife replied, ' *Yes,*'—and I
heard no more.

"How shall I tell you the rest? I could scarcely breathe ; my whole body was as cold as marble ;
to have seen me, you could not have told whether
I was dead or alive. Heavens! when I yet think
upon it! We two were almost without arms ;—
against us were twelve or fifteen who had plenty
of weapons. And then my comrade dead of sleep
and fatigue ! To call him up, to make a noise, was
more than I dared ;—to escape alone was an impossibility. The window was not very high, but
under it were two great dogs howling like wolves.
Imagine if you can, the distress I was in. At the
end of a quarter of an hour, which seemed an age,
I heard some one on the staircase, and through the
chink of the door I saw the old man, with a lamp
in one hand, and one of his great knives in the
other. He mounted, his wife after him ; I was behind the door. He opened it ; but before he came
in he put down the lamp, which his wife took up,
and coming in with his feet naked, she being behind him said, with a smothered voice, hiding the
light partially with her fingers, ' *Gently, go gently.*'
When he reached the ladder he mounted, his knife
between his teeth ; and going to the head of the

bed where that poor young man lay, with his throat uncovered, and with one hand he took his knife, and with the other——ah, my cousin——he seized a ham which hung down from the roof, cut a slice, and retired as he had come in. The door is re-shut, the light vanishes, and I am left alone to my reflections.

" When the day appeared, all the family with a great noise came to rouse us, as we had desired. They brought us plenty to eat, they served us a very proper breakfast—a capital breakfast, I assure you. Two capons formed part of it, of which, said the hostess, you must eat one, and carry away the other. When I saw the capons I at once comprehended the meaning of those terrible words— ' *Must we kill them both ?*' "

## THE ALPINE HERD BOY.

IN Switzerland, among the Alps, in a low-eaved cot, lived Peter, the herd-boy of Monsieur Vattêmal, a rich landholder in a neighboring valley. This gentleman had but one child, a son, born a week later than Peter. As his mother died soon after, the child was given to the herd-boy's mother to be nursed. Hippolyte was delicate, Peter hardy. It was a pretty sight when the latter led his foster brother by the hand up the side of the mountain.

For five years they lived in the same cot, partook of the same fare, and little suspected the difference of their lot. M. Vattêmal brought a lovely bride to the valley, and one pleasant eve, his char-â-banc stopped at the cot, while Peter's mother hastened, with fast falling tears, to meet the parents of her foster child, knowing too well that they were come to take him from her. Hippolyte left the cot that evening. His father was gratified to see the good effect of his mountain life. Although more delicate and graceful than Peter, his constitution was sound and his motions vigorous. The children now dwelt a mile apart, but often met. When Peter was eight years old, M. Vattêmal gave him lessons with his son. At the age of twelve Hippolyte was sent to Geneva to be fitted for college, while to Peter was given the situation of herd-boy. The sterling principles of truth and honesty, early grafted in his character, made him quite worthy of the place he filled.

Most of the Swiss peasants knit while tending their flocks—Peter studied. Although M. Vattêmal thought that four years' schooling was enough for the herd-boy, Peter did not. He resolved at fourteen to open an evening-school in his mother's kitchen. Many of the mountaineers had expressed a wish to learn to read. They deemed Peter a fortunate and learned lad. His mother was astonished, but would not refuse him. As soon as the long evenings commenced, he opened his school. It was successful. He not only had the pleasure of teaching many to read, but found their remuneration, when collected, quite ample, although each gave but a small sum. For three years he was a faithful herd-boy, but at the opening of the fourth year informed M. Vattêmal that he was going to Geneva, as a traveler, who met and traveled with him on the mountains, had given him the address of the principal of a large academy there, who would, perhaps, instruct him in the higher branches of learning as payment for Peter's services. M. Vattêmal listened with much interest.

"So, my lad, you despise the lot of a herd-boy."

"Sir," replied Peter, "I despise no lot, but aspire to one higher. In this book I now hold, I have learned how the poorest and humblest citizens of America attain, by patient industry, to a sphere far higher than that they were born in."

"Ah, my young man! pray who lent you this wonderful book?"

"An American traveler met me on the mountains. I was reading the life of Fenelon—a present from your son—when he spoke to me. Before we parted he told me of Monsieur Carday's establishment, and urged me to go to him. He called upon me twice after our interview, and gave me this book, with a letter of introduction to M. Carday."

M. Vattêmal took the volume, and read the name of the giver on the fly-leaf.

"One of the greatest statesmen of America—of the world!"

"Sir!" cried Peter, surprised at his employer's emotion.

"Peter," said that gentleman, "the friend who gave you this book has one of the greatest intellects that ever made a nation glorious. Obey your monitor; go to M. Carday. I will take you part of the way, and assist you with my purse."

"Sir," replied Peter, with a blush of gratitude suffusing his face, "I have means. May I ask you to use the sum destined for me, to aid our mountaineers?"

"It shall be as you wish."

"The Chamois hunter, Rogernoir, is quite disabled by a recent fall——"

"I understand you, my noble lad. I will employ the fund destined for you, in behalf of his family."

Peter withdrew with firm tread. As he walked to the gate a monarch might envy the majestic step of the high-souled herd-boy. His mother met him. The few articles they owned were packed snugly in one corner. As Peter's eyes rested wonderingly on this arrangement, his mother whispered—

"I shall not part with you, my son."

"Dearest mother!" he could say so more.

"I have a distant relative, a pastry cook, in Geneva. I shall find employment, and be near my son."

In two days they departed. M. Vattêmal escorted them more than half way. As he parted from them he slipped a purse into the mother's hand, and whispered—

"From Hippolyte, to his foster mother."

The pastry cook was quite pleased to see his cousin. His wife, with the help of Hippolyte's

THE ALPS.

purse, soon arrayed the peasant in suitable apparel. The herd-boy's mother was comely and well-bred, so that her city friends were quite pleased with her. They lived very near M. Carday. That gentleman was happy to oblige his American friend. Peter was to teach the lesser boys, and in return receive instructions from the best masters. His time was almost constantly occupied, save the few hours spent with his mother. Sometimes they rambled on the shores of Lake Geneva, or took an ice in one of the public gardens. Peter wrote a good hand. He earned some francs by copying, at odd intervals, law papers for a friend of M. Carday. It was one fine Sabbath eve as they walked by the lake, that Peter informed his mother of his determination to go to America, and become a lawyer. The chance of success in Geneva, without patronage, was so small that Peter resolved not to hope for it. As before, his mother's only answer was a decision to go with him. M. Vattêmal was consulted ; he gave his approval with a sum sufficient to defray their expenses. In a month after they left Geneva. M. Vattêmal received a letter written by Peter immediately after their arrival in Boston. The rich landholder was sitting with his family on the balcony when the letter was brought in. Hippolyte, now an exquisite of the first water, was smoking. The father looked up at his son as he finished reading the letter.

Alas, thought he, what would I not give if my light-headed son could write such a manly letter as this. But Hippylite will be a dandy until he is a father ; then he will become a nobody.

In Boston Peter presented his few letters. He

hired three rooms in a pleasant location, and soon had several pupils to whom he taught German and French. His mother found ample employment.— She was a skillful basket-maker. Her toys met rapid sale, as they were quite unique in Boston. She also netted well. She followed the advice of some female friends, and exchanged a room for a small shop in the building. This was soon filled with articles furnished by her indefatigable friends. Her son assisted her to arrange the goods tastefully; her nets, toys, and baskets, were soon added to by an accomplishment learned of her cousin, the pastry cook. These articles of cookery became famous. As Peter went up step by step to his goal, his mother with a bound attained her's, for her shop was enlarged and her success permanent. She assisted her son with funds, and at last, with sparkling eyes, read the letter in which he informed M. Vattêmal that he was now a lawyer. That gentleman was just concluding a marriage treaty for Hippolyte when he received the news.

So, thought he, my son is an empty-headed roué, while the herd-boy is a lawyer—a man of intellect, with a noble soul. "Nature makes no distinctions."

Mr. W——, the traveler amid the Alps, had been a true friend to Peter. By his advice the mother and son moved westward. They had been frugal and industrious. This was the only magic that had given them sufficient means to go to Michigan and purchase a house on the shore of one of the lakes, not far from a large town. The dwelling was a plain, two-story house with three acres of rich land surrounding it. In the town Peter hired an office; as he understood conveyancing well he soon found business. His letters introduced him to good society; his polished manners enabled him to keep his place in it. His mother supplied two toy shops with products of Swiss origin, and with those delicious articles she learned to make at Geneva. Her income was quite large, as some of the towns adjacent heard of her skill, and sent weekly to the Lake-house, as it was called, for her products. Yet few persons, save the shopkeepers, knew that she made the confections so famous with old and young.

Peter was very successful, because skillful and upright. He married soon after the death of Hippolyte, who was drowned while bathing in the Arve. M. Vattêmal had now quite a family. The letters of Peter aroused his ambition to settle his children well. Every avenue to business in Switzerland was so thronged as to discourage him from attempting to place them advantageously. Hippolyte's wife and child had been laid in the family vault, before the rapid waters of the Arve flung his lifeless corpse on the pebbly shore. M. Vattêmal astonished Peter by suddenly appearing at the Lake-house. The beauty of the environs and cheapness of land pleased M. Vattêmal. He concluded to purchase a farm adjoining Peter's estate, and soon had the satisfaction of installing his family in their new home. Peter's wife and mother were true friends to Madame Vattêmal, who was long in becoming acquainted with the language and manners of her adopted country. M. Vattêmal had the satisfaction of seeing his sons suitably embarked in business. One of them became in time Peter's partner, and to the wise training of Peter owed much of his sagacity in his profession.

Time brought many changes to the environs of the Lake-house. Peter remained the same, save the usual marks of age. Simple in his habits, even in his temperament, and pious in his feelings, he became a centre of attraction to old and young. The plain stone dwelling betrayed none of that love of change too frequently seen in this country. It was unaltered since he first purchased it. The Lake-house was long noted for its hospitality. Music was not neglected; Peter played well on the organ and flageolet. His wife was a good musician. She delighted to gather the young people on the lawn, and treat them to fine strawberries. As Peter was known to be wealthy, his children too often felt the homage paid to riches. When he perceived any tokens of pride in them he would say—

"Do you see that picture over the chimney-piece? The boy represented there, as sitting on a rock with sheep near him, his hat torn by rough mountain winds, his feet bare, and his clothes patched, is now your father. As you see him there, so he looked when herd-boy for M. Vattėmal."

## A CONVERSATION ABOUT ISLANDS.

ONE fine morning in August, Henry, Mary, and Robert, started with their father, for a sail down the Bay of New York, and a visit at their cousin's on Staten Island.

As the steamer moved quietly over the water, they had a beautiful view of the harbor and of the scenery in passing down the Bay, and they were all in the best of spirits.

Now, the city is fast receding from their view, its tall steeples are fading in the distance, and the wilderness of its masts seem like a dense forest of pines.

On the left is the beautiful Long Island shore, with its pretty cottages and highly cultivated fields—Greenwood, the city of the dead, and Fort Hamilton, commanding from its elevation, one of the finest water views that the world affords.

On the left, and far astern, is the dim outline of the highlands, and nearer, is the New Jersey shore, scolloped with bays, and inlets, and nearer still is

Staten Island, about which the children are making a thousand inquiries, until at length the conversation turns on the subject of islands in general.

"Which is the largest island on the globe?" said Robert.

"Australia, or New Holland, which is large enough to be a continent, being more than twenty-four times as large as the island of Great Britain."

"It is very large," said Henry, "but it does not join any other land, and I suppose that is the reason it is not called a continent; which you told us means 'holding together.'"

"There are a great many islands," said Mary, "between Australia and the continent of Asia. I suppose if they were joined they would be a continent."

"That large cluster of islands is called the Indian Archipelago," said her father. "It is one of the hottest regions in the world, lying immediately under the equator. It is also a region of volcanoes. In one of the islands called Sumbawa, an eruption occurred in 1815, which was of a very astonishing kind, on account of the distance to which the noise and the trembling of the earth extended, and also on account of the fury of the eruption, which destroyed thousands of individuals."

"The trembling could not reach beyond the island itself, I suppose?" said Henry, "because there must be water all around it."

"A group of islands, like that archipelago, no doubt forms part of a chain of mountains stretching out from the continent, the *upper* portions of which only are visible above the waters. Thus an earthquake or volcanic eruption at one part of the chain would be felt in another part. This was the case among these islands; the earthquakes at Sumbawa being felt at the distance of a thousand miles in every direction, while the explosions were distinctly heard in the island of Sumatra, which cannot be less than a thousand miles from the spot. The showers of volcanic ashes were so prodigious, that at Java, three hundred miles off, total darkness was produced at mid-day."

The children thought that the bed of the ocean must be wonderfully deep, to allow of mountain-chains in it whose tops only should rise above the waters, and Henry asked whether such islands are barren places, such as the tops of mountains generally are.

"Some of the smaller islands of the ocean are mere rocks," said his father, "and have evidently been thrown up by the eruptions of submarine volcanoes. But the others, though hilly, have also rich valleys and plains, and are in many cases extremely fertile."

Mary had been looking at the map while her papa was speaking of the islands of the Indian Archipelago, and she said she should be sorry to live in hot countries, for the volcanoes seemed all to be there.

"You forget," said Henry, "that papa told us there were several in Kamtschatka, which is a terribly cold place."

MOUNT VESUVIUS.

"There are also numerous volcanoes," said his father, "in the island of the Northern Ocean called Iceland; so that coldness of climate does not form a protection from these terrible visitations. The whole of that island appears to have been formed by volcanic agency."

"After all," said Henry, "I think the volcanoes are of some use in the world, if they send up islands for people to live on. I did not know before that they were useful."

"People had much better not live in such dangerous places," said Mary. "If such an island were to rise up in our seas I would not even set my foot on it, much less live on it."

"But some of the volcanoes go out and do not burn any longer," said Robert. "The island must be safe enough then, and it would be foolish to be afraid of it because it was once a volcano."

"If you were to see some of the beautiful islands of the South Seas," said her father, "you would change your opinion, as to their not being fit to live in. Here is a picture of one of them, and you see that the mountains have been thrown into picturesque forms, which are evidently produced by volcanoes, although there is no sign of any recent eruption. The slopes and valleys of many of these islands are very beautiful, and the soil on them is very fertile. But these islands are not all of volcanic origin, thrown up by violent eruptions from the bowels of the earth; a geological examination of them shows conclusively that many of them are of coral formation—that their formation is nothing else than immense coral rocks, rising up from the bed of the ocean, and covered by a gradual process with soil, and thus fitted up as a beautiful dwelling place for man. These coral formations are constantly going on beneath the surface of the water. In many places there are now immense coral reefs rising up, so as to be dangerous when they lie in the pathway of ships. Ere long they will rise above the surface of the water. All these coral mountains beneath the sea and rising above the sea,

A VOLCANIC ISLAND.

so beautiful are the work of a people, that like bees are industriously plying their art and producing the most astonishing results."

"Rocks and islands of coral!" said Mary. "How wonderful! how beautiful! Is it red or white coral? Do, papa, tell us more about them. You spoke as if some one was always at work building them. Who is it? and where does he get the coral from? If I knew him I would ask him for some nice large pieces to put in our cabinet."

"The architects of the coral rocks are not persons with whom you can hold any communication," said her papa, with a smile: "and yet, such wonderful skill and power has God bestowed upon them, that they are able not only to raise a coral rock in the middle of the sea, but also to make the coral itself of which the work is composed."

The children looked at their father in amazement; and Henry said it was the strangest thing he had ever heard of. "If people were going to build a palace for the queen," said he, "the architects would have first to get the stone and the marble somewhere; for they could not make them; and how is it possible that these other builders should be able to make the stones themselves for the coral islands, and such beautiful ones too, out in the middle of the sea?"

"I wish they would come and work on land," said Mary, "we might then have coral palaces."

Robert saw that his papa was smiling, and it suddenly came into his head, that the architects of the coral rocks might not be men after all.

"Oh, papa," said he, "I do not think you mean a real architect, but some creature that builds the rock, as bees do their cells, and perhaps collects the coral somewhere as bees do their honey."

"You are partly right and partly wrong," said his father, "coral rocks are produced by vast multitudes of sea animals, commonly called *coral insects*. They are not, however, insects, but very small soft-bodied animals, resembling little bags of jelly. At the end of this bag are six or eight little arms or feelers. Coral itself is not collected by these little animals as you fancy, but is produced in some wonderful manner from their own bodies. They form stone cells beneath the waves for their own abode; and owing to the countless millions employed upon the task, they gradually raise a vast structure of coral, all united in one mass, and forming at length an island fitted for man."

"I wonder the rough waves of the sea do not wash away the stones and the builders, too, and so put an end to their work," said Henry.

"It is one of the most astonishing facts in nature," said his father, "that these little, soft, jelly-like creatures, are able to work on in the midst of the ocean, and to build a fabric which is strong enough to resist the violence of the breakers. It teaches us that among all the works of God there is nothing to be thought likely of, or considered insignificant. The meanest insect may be designed by its Maker to perform some important task in the world, which man, perhaps, would be quite unable to accomplish."

"And do the coral insects begin building at the bottom of the sea, and work on till they get to the top?" said Henry.

"By asking that question, Henry, you have started a difficulty," said his father. "Coral islands are found in seas three hundred fathoms deep, and yet the coral animal cannot exist at a greater depth in the sea than about twenty fathoms.* Therefore, during the great changes in the earth's surface which I have already spoken of, the level of the sea must either have been lower when these animals began to build, or else we must suppose them to have laid their foundation on submarine rocks, within twenty fathoms of the surface. On some of these islands the coral rocks appear to have been forcibly raised above the surface of the waters; for, I should tell you, that the builders themselves never work above the waves. The ocean is their element, and in it they live and die."

"The islands, as these creatures make them, must be stony and barren places," said Henry. "How do they become fit for people to live on?"

"The waves of the sea throw up fragments of the rock itself, together with shells and sand, on the surface of the island, and these soon form a soil for the seeds which are conveyed on the waters

* A fathom is six feet.

from distant places. Mosses, and other small plants, soon clothe the dazzling white surface of the coral; and sometimes entire trunks of trees are wafted thither from other shores, bearing with them the eggs and insects, as the first contribution towards peopling the surface. Sea-birds soon make a resting-place of the island; and when trees and bushes begin to spring up, strayed land-birds also find shelter therein. Thus does the soil become gradually fit for the use of man, though the process may be extremely slow, by which all these changes are effected."

"Where are these wonderful coral islands to be found?" asked Mary.

"Chiefly in the Pacific Ocean, which is distinguished from all other seas by the vast number of its islands."

"But they are not all coral islands, are they, papa?"

"Not all, perhaps; but the greater part are so," replied her father; "some of the coral islands are very low, being nothing more than curved belts of rocks, rising a yard or two above the surface of the water, and enclosing a portion of the sea, which is called a *lagoon*, or lake. These coral formations frequently enclose not only a large lagoon, but several small islands. Many of them extend, in an irregular curve, to the length of ten or twenty miles, the width of the reef of rocks not being more than half a mile. These rocks are covered with the most luxuriant vegetation, and the feathery foliage of the cocoa-nut tree waves gracefully in the trade wind. The coral shores are of dazzling whiteness."

"These islands must be very beautiful," said Mary; "but I should not like their being so low."

"You would like those better, that papa said had been lifted up by some means," said Henry.

"Mary would not think them so beautiful," said her father, "for although they are more elevated they have fewer trees. Some of the rocks have been forced up from one hundred to five hundred feet above the water's edge. These bear marks of having once been coral rocks, but by the action of the weather, they are now much harder and brighter than coral, and the islands formed by them are called crystal islands. Some of them have beautiful caverns, the roofs of which are composed of crystalized coral. Such islands are not very numerous.

"Before we leave the subject of islands," continued their father, "I must tell you that the volcanic islands are protected from the waves by a reef of coral, and sometimes this reef is a mile and a half, or two miles from the beach. In the case of an island called Bolabola, the reef extends like a ring round the island, and is sufficiently raised above the waters to produce groves of cocoa-nut trees. The openings in the reefs of the larger islands are generally opposite the mouth of a river.

"You see in the cut, a beautiful view of Bolabola, surrounded with its ring-like reef on which the cocoa-nut trees are growing. What a contrast between the low islands with their luxuriant foliage and fruit, and the bold cliff that rises like a steeple to the sky, and looks as though it had defied the storms and hurricanes of centuries!"

BOLABOLA.

"What are hurricanes?" asked Robert.

"They are terrific storms of wind, often rushing

from different quarters at the same time, and committing frightful devastation."

"But what do they do, papa?" said Robert.

"They tear up trees by the roots, and overthrow houses and churches, occasioning great loss of property, and sometimes of life. They are often very destructive in the West India Islands, and indeed in all the tropics."

By this time the boat approached the landing on Staten Island, where our happy little party were to go ashore, and the conversation, in which they all had been so much interested, was brought to a close.

It was no new thing to them to enter into such little instructive discussions. The children were eager to know all about the subjects of which they read, and their father was most happy to answer their inquiries, and to gratify their desire for useful knowledge.

If it is our privilege ever to be present at another of their cozy conversations, you, my young friends, shall be informed of what they say.

## THE MAN WITH THE IRON MASK.

N the reign of Louis the Fourteenth, a mysterious captive, with his face concealed by a black mask, was confined successively in the fortress of Pignerol, in that of the Isle of Saint Marguerite, and lastly in the Bastile. His imprisonment included a period of twenty-four years, during which he was always in custody of the Signor de St. Mars, who was consecutively the commandant or governor of all these fortresses. In April, 1687, the masked prisoner was brought from Pignerol to St. Marguerite, which is an island in the Mediterranean on the coast of Provence. He was carried in a chair so closely covered with oil-cloth as to conceal him entirely; eight men were in attendance to carry it in turn, being accompanied by a guard of soldiers and St. Mars the governor. His island prison was a room in one of the towers of the fortress facing the north, lighted by a single window set in a very thick stone wall. This casement was guarded by bars of iron and looked out upon the sea—and here he remained in rigid confinement for eleven years.

It has been related that, while imprisoned in this place, the unknown captive wrote something with a knife upon one of his silver plates and threw the plate from the window, towards a boat which was moored near the foot of the tower. A fisherman picked up the plate and honestly carried it to the governor, who, much surprised, inquired if he had read the writing upon it. "I do not know how to read," answered the fisherman; "I have just found the plate, and no one else has seen it." He was, nevertheless, detained within the fort for several days; and, when dismissing him with a reward, the governor said, "Go, you are very fortunate in not knowing how to read."

It is also asserted that, on another occasion, the prisoner wrote all over a fine shirt, which was seen floating on the water just under his window, by a friar of this island. This priest was so conscientious as to carry it directly to St. Mars, who pressed him eagerly to tell him if he had read it. Though the friar positively denied having done so, yet knowing that he of course was able to read, the governor still doubted his veracity. Two days afterwards this friar was found dead in his bed.

In the autumn of 1698, the unknown captive was transferred to the Bastile, of which St. Mars was appointed commandant. The journey from the southern coast of France to the city of Paris was, in those days, a very long one. The mysterious prisoner was carried in a litter, a closely-curtained vehicle slung between two horses. The litter was guarded by soldiers on horseback and accompanied by the carriage of Saint Mars, at whose own estate of Palteau—which was near the road—they passed a night and part of two days.

The prisoner was of tall stature and remarkably fine figure. His face was covered by a mask of black velvet, strengthened and shaped with whalebone, and fastened behind with a small padlock, of which St. Mars, always kept the key. This mask was erroneously reported to be made of iron, and the belief became so general—notwithstanding the impossibility of any human being continuing long in existence with a covering of that metal perpetually on his face—that "the man with the iron mask" is the appellation by which this unfortunate personage has always been distinguished. The name by which St. Mars addressed him was Marchiali: but it was understood to be fictitious, and merely adopted because of the necessity that those about him should, for their own convenience, call him something.

During the journey from St. Marguerite to Paris, the governor always sat opposite to him at table, with a loaded pistol on each side of his plate, that he might shoot the prisoner in case he attempted to discover himself, even to the single domestic that waited on them at meals. The dishes were left in the ante-room, and brought to the eating-department by this servant, who carefully locked the door whenever he came in. A bed was put up for St. Mars, close to that of his charge, that he might keep him in view during the night.

In the afternoon that they arrived at the Bastile the masked captive was immediately shut up in one of the lower rooms; but at nine in the evening he was conducted by Dujonca, the king's lieutenant—who relates the circumstance—to an apartment prepared for him in that part of the building called the Bertaudiere tower, where he wore away the last five years of his melancholy existence. His face was always concealed by the black mask, and never seen even by his physician. He was evidently of a dark or brown complexion, and his hair was tinged with gray. His skin was extremely fine and smooth, and his voice remarkably agreeable. He was only permitted to speak to the governor St. Mars, to Rosarges the major-domo, to Reilh the surgeon, and to Girault the chaplain of the Bastile. He was allowed sometimes to hear mass in the chapel of that fortress, passing thither through the court-yard between a line of soldiers, all ranged with their muskets presented, and having orders to fire on him if he spoke. He read much in the solitude of his tower, and was frequently heard to play on the guitar.

The prisoner with the mask died in the Bastile, on the 19th of November, 1703, after a few hours' illness; expiring so suddenly that the chaplain, who was sent for to administer the last sacrament, had only time to address a few words to his parting spirit. The date of his arrival at the Bastile under the name of Marchiah, with the day and hour of his death, were regularly registered on the archive of that gloomy prison, and respected long after by many persons whose curiosity led them to examine into the few facts that glimmer through the mist which will most probably rest forever on his history.

On the day that followed the close of his life and sufferings, the body of the unknown captive was wrapped in a winding sheet of fine new linen, and interred in the cemetery of St. Paul's Church in Paris. There is a tradition of a gentleman having bribed the sexton to open the grave and allow him to look at the corpse of Marchiali the night after its burial. On removing the coffin lid it was found the head was not there, a stone being in place of it.

Immediately after the death of the prisoner, orders were received at the Bastile to destroy every thing that had been used in his service. His clothes, bedding, and bedstead were burnt, as were the tables and chairs belonging to his room; the window frame and the door were burnt also. Whatever was made of silver or any other metal was melted down, and some articles were pounded to powder, even the glass of his window and his mirror. The tiles that paved the floor were all taken up lest he should have concealed under them something that might lead to the disclosure of his real name and story; everything beneath was carefully scraped away, and the pavement replaced by a new one. Even the ceiling was taken away and replaced by another; the walls were also plastered anew. It was obvious that great apprehensions were entertained of his having left some indications which might tend to the discovery of a secret, that even after death was never to be disclosed.

For more than a century, conjecture has been busy as to the true history of this remarkable prisoner, about whom so many extraordinary precautions were taken by the government of France; various theories being adopted concerning his identity, with numerous conjectures as to the cause of his long and rigorous captivity, and the unremitting concealment of his face. Very plausible evidence has been adduced—particularly within the last few years—to show that the person called the man with the iron mask could be no other than Count Matthioli, the confidential secretary and first minister of Charles Ferdinand duke of Mantua. With this Prince, Louis the Fourteenth had entered into a private negotiation for the purchase of his chief city. But the faithful secretary dissuaded the duke of Mantua from selling any part of his dominions, and induced him to break off the treaty and unite himself with the other princes of Italy in oppressing and curbing the ambitious encroachments of the king of France. Count Matthioli went to Rome, Venice, Geneva, and other Italian states, and succeeded so well as to detach them all from the interest of France; and he finally repaired to Turin with the same intention. The French government, however, had been secretly informed of all these missions, and was therefore highly incensed against the Mantuan minister. Now that he was so near the territories of the king of France, a design was formed to entrap him for punishment, and by shutting him up in secret to prevent his farther interference with any plans against Italy. Marshal Catinat—who commanded the French troops in that part of the frontier—invited Matthioli to a meeting in the vicinity of Pignerol. Here Catinat awaited him with some officers and soldiers; and, contrary to the law of nations, Matthioli, the subject and minister of a foreign prince, was immediately arrested, and conducted to the fortress of Pignerol, which was the commencement of his long and strict captivity. His wife retired to a convent of nuns in Bologna.

That the man with the iron mask was Count Matthioli is the latest, and probably the truest explanation of a mystery which perhaps will never be more clearly elucidated. This opinion was first suggested about sixty years ago, and has been recently revived. The belief generally prevailing throughout the last century, regarded the unknown captive—for the concealment of whose identity such extraordinary precautions were taken both when living and dead—as a person of much higher rank and consequence than the secretary of an Italian prince.

Voltaire, and other writers, asserted their conviction that the man with the iron mask was in reality a twin brother of Louis the Fourteenth. According to their statement, it had been reported at court that a herdsman who professed the power of prophecy, had predicted that if tnere should be two dauphins in France, their rival claims to the throne would convulse the whole kingdom and deluge it in blood. The rage of superstition had not yet gone by.

On the birth of the twin princes the expedient was adopted of concealing one of them, but keeping him alive in case the death of his brother should leave the crown without an heir, and make it expedient to produce him. He was, therefore, sent to a remote place at the southern extremity of the kingdom, and there brought up in secret; while his more fortunate brother was presented to the world as dauphin of France and successor to the throne.

The story goes that after the rejected prince had grown up, the resemblance of his features to those of his brother—who was now Louis the Fourteenth—became so striking, as to make it dangerous to allow him to be seen, lest the truth should be guessed and a party raised in his favor. It was, therefore, considered expedient to cover his face with a perpetual mask, and to shut him up for life, in the custody of one who could be trusted with the secret.

Voltaire's version of the story of the man with the iron mask, whether true or false, has always been the most popular; and he hints being in the confidence of some one who owns the facts. It seems to offer the best explanation for the importance that was certainly attached to the prisoner; for the concealment of his features; for the unremitting closeness with which he was watched while living; and for the apprehensions of discovery which even his death could not allay. It is supposed that both the Fifteenth and Sixteenth Louis were acquainted with the secret, and that it is probably known to the few surviving descendants of the old royal family of France.

## TRAVELS ABOUT AFRICA.

PROBABLY most of our readers think of Africa as a country famous for black people with curly hair, thick lips and flat noses—a capital place for deserts and all sorts of wild beasts—a land where you may get plenty of elephants' teeth and plenty of gold dust—where you will see fierce lions and tigers and birds of beautiful plumage—and where, if you have a fancy for the thing, you may journey on an ostrich's back with almost incredible rapidity—a land where you may be broiled to death by the sun, smothered with the hot burning sand, die of thirst in the pathless desert, be eaten up by tigers or swallowed alive by a huge snake. If you have a relish for any of these, or for some genuine Gilbert Go-ahead adventures, we advise you to start off directly for Africa. We will warrant that your adventures will not lack thrilling interest and startling variety. Perhaps some of our young readers will be induced to take a tour, and write home an account of their discoveries. We do not intend to forestall any such undertaking by writing an extended article on Africa, but will confine ourselves to a few generalities.

Africa is a country marked by striking contrasts. Some portions of it were the first to be explored and occupied by man, while others remain to the present day unexplored and unknown regions. In

early ages, it was the seat and centre of learning and science, while now, the most of its inhabitants are shrouded in intellectual and moral darkness. Africa presents the most remarkable contrast of fertility and desolation ; the valley of the Nile is the garden of the world, while the wastes of Sahara are proverbial for their desolation.

In surveying its civil and social condition, we see the negroes, a weak and harmless race, made the prey of the Arab, the most despotic and remorseless of the human family.

The lion, the leopard, and the panther, feasting upon the vast herds of antelopes that graze over the central wastes of Africa, afford a striking analogy to human society—the weak, the timid, and the defenceless, being made, without mercy or scruple, the prey of the daring and the strong.

The prevailing aspect of the country in Africa is rude, gloomy and sterile. It may be considered as in all respects the least favored quarter of the globe. Its immense deserts, exposed to the vertical rays of a tropical sun, are deprived of all the moisture necessary to cover them with vegetation. Moving sands, tossed by wind, and whirled in eddies, surround and often bury the traveler. The best known and most fertile portion of Africa is that which borders upon the Mediterranean Sea. The least known regions are the central portions into whose depths no traveler has yet thoroughly penetrated; but it is the general impression of travelers, founded on partial explorations, that there are immense territories of fine land in the interior of Africa—that they enjoy a healthful climate, and are populated by a large and not unlikely an intelligent people, whose entire history is as yet unknown to the world. We do not know from actual discovery, that there are many tribes in the inland territories greatly superior to those inhabiting the coasts.

The portions of central Africa that have been

TRAVEL AND ADVENTURE. 103

explored, have been found to be full of interest. They abound in varied and wonderful scenery, and are inhabited by tribes of varied character and habits. These tribes are quite distinct from each other, and as diversified in their tastes and habits

as you can imagine. We cannot better illustrate this fact than by wood-cut representations of local African chiefs introduced in this article. They seem to be arrayed in full costume, and, to their uncultivated taste, their adorning doubtless appears very becoming.

In the moral existence of those portions of central Africa that have been explored, there are many very dark features. War is carried on with all the ferocity of the most barbarous nations; tribe is arrayed against tribe, and the territory of the conquered is made a desolation and a waste. Yet it must not be concluded that an unbroken gloom hangs over the moral condition of Africa. There seems to be something peculiarly engaging and amiable in the social feelings and habits there prevalent.

When Mungo Park was traveling in central Africa, he arrived one night at Sego, in Bambarra, but the king was suspicious of him, and forbade him to advance and cross the river. Under these circumstances, he was obliged to return and lodge in a distant village. But there the same distrust of the white man prevailed, and no person would allow him to enter his house. He says, " I was regarded with astonishment and fear, and was obliged to sit without food under the shade of a tree. The wind arose, and there was a great appearance of a heavy rain; and the wild beasts were so numerous in the neighborhood, that I should have been obliged to take shelter among the branches of the trees.

About sunset, as I was preparing to pass the night in this manner, and had turned my horse loose that he might graze at liberty, a woman returning from the labors of the field, stopped to observe me. Perceiving that I was weary and dejected, she inquired into my situation, which I briefly explained to her; whereupon, with looks of great compassion, she took up my saddle and bridle and bade me follow her. Having conducted me into her hut, she lighted a lamp, spread a mat on the floor and told me I might remain there for the night. Finding that I was hungry, she went out and soon returned with a very fine fish, which being broiled upon some embers, she gave me for supper. The women then resumed their labors of spinning cotton, and lightened their labor with songs, one of which must have been composed extempore, for I was myself the subject of it. It was sung by one of the young women, the rest joining in a kind of chorus. The air was sweet and plaintive, and the words, literally translated, were these:—

> "The winds roared, and the rains fell;
> The poor white man, faint and weary,
> Came and sat under our tree.
> He has no mother to bring him milk,
> No wife to grind his corn.
>
> CHORUS.
>
> Let us pity the white man,
> No mother has he to bring him milk,
> No wife to grind his corn."

The reader can fully sympathize with this intelligent traveler, when he observes, " trifling as this recital may appear, the circumstance was highly affecting to a person in my situation. I was oppressed with such unaffected kindness, and sleep fled from my eyes. In the morning I presented my compassionate landlady with two of the four brass buttons remaining on my waistcoat, the only recompense I could make her."

So far as observations have extended, the people in central Africa are rude in their tastes and extremely uncultivated in all their habits and feelings. The dress and ornaments indicated by the costume of the chiefs as in the above cuts, marks a barbarous age, and shows that whatever qualities they may possess, there is ample room for civilization and Christianity to work improvement, and it is an interesting feature of the present times that great interest is felt among all Christian people in the regeneration of Africa. Almost every denomination of Christians is sending missionaries among them. The coasts are being occupied by intelligent and thriving settlers, commerce with other nations is every year extended and enlarged, towns and cities are springing up, schools are started, and churches are built, and all the blessings of a well ordered government are being rapidly introduced.

While the coast is thus being occupied with Christian colonies and Africa is being surrounded with a belt of light, constant explorations are made into the interior, and the day may not be distant when Africa will come up to take her place among the nations, and in her advancement be honored and blessed.

## THE HIGHLANDS OF SCOTLAND.

SCOTLAND, occupying the northern portion of Great Britain, is separated from England by a series of hills and rivers, and is distinguished from that country by many peculiar features.

Bold mountain chains form a large portion of the surface, giving occasion for many deep inlets of the sea, and rendering the general outline extremely irregular.

Lakes embosomed in the hills, and clear and rapid rivers pouring along the vales, help to complete the picture sketched by a native poet—

> "Land of the mountain and the flood,
> Land of brown heath and shaggy wood."

The north of Scotland bears the general name of Highlands, and may be considered as one great cluster of hills interspersed with deep precipices, rushing streams, and romantic lakes, and forming altogether some of the most wild and imposing scenery in the world.

To one familiar with the mountain and lake scenery of America, there is not much of novelty in the mountains and lakes of the Highlands, except that the former appear more bald and bleak, and the latter more clear and tranquil. As you pass over their smooth water you seem to look into

# TRAVEL AND ADVENTURE. 109

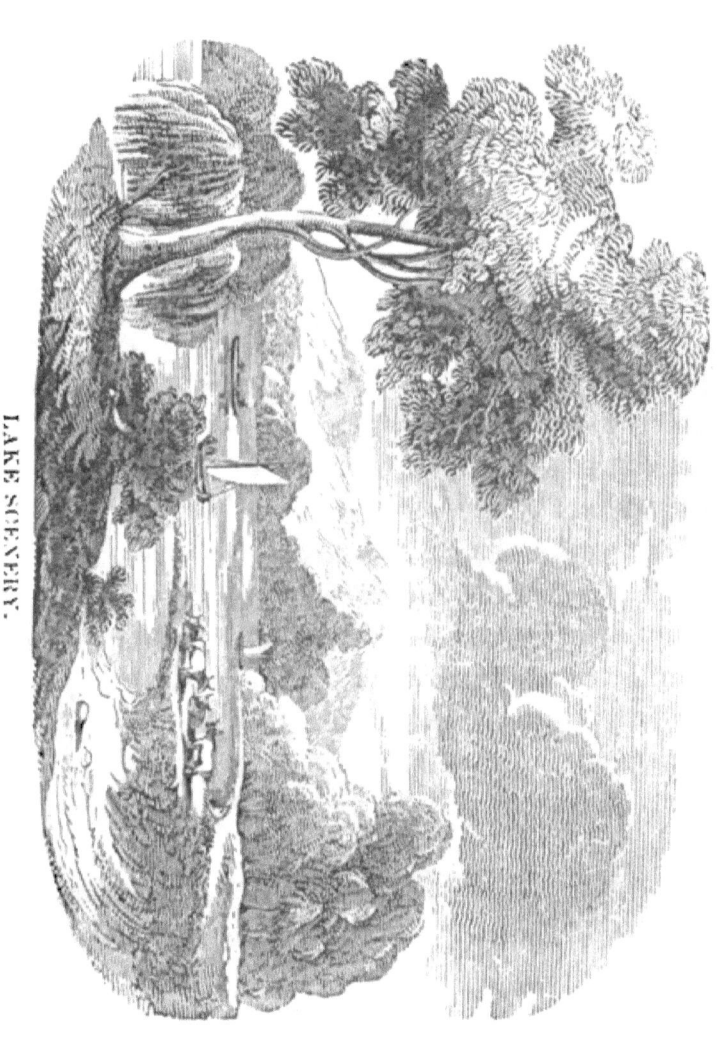

LAKE SCENERY.

its deepest depth, and discern its pebbly bottom, and you cannot but admire the beautiful images formed on its mirrored surface by the shadows of the surrounding hills. You will also be attracted by the irregular form and bold outline of the lake shores—here is a deep-shaded inlet, and there is a bold headland jutting out into the water.

The Highland country embraces about one-sixth of the entire population of Scotland. The inhabitants are of Celtic descent, and exhibit many striking peculiarities of feature, language, dress, and manners. The history of the Highlanders in the earlier days of Scotland is full of bold and romantic adventure, and has formed the theme of many a song and story.

The remainder of the country of Scotland is termed the Lowlands, and is less irregular, but here the surface is varied by hill and valley and several mountain ranges. The inhabitants are, like the English, a Teutonic people, but with a mixture of Celtic blood, and are distinguished for their intelligence, industry, and great energy of character.

A country, with so many physical disadvantages could never have been brought into such a condition as respects rural husbandry, or been made so prosperous a seat of manufacture and commerce, unless the people were highly gifted with a spirit of enterprise.

TRAVEL AND ADVENTURE. 111

In the poorest districts we nowhere meet with the destitution and wretchedness that are found in

Ireland; on the contrary, there is an air of comfort in their lowly dwellings.

Caution, foresight, and reflection, enter largely into the Scottish character, hence they are slow and sometimes apparently cold, and appear to be deficient in frankness and generosity.

But these qualities are only seeming—they are a people of generous and warm-hearted affections —ardently attached to their country and to the spot that gave them birth, and keenly alive to every thing that reminds them of what is honorable and chivalric in the doings of their ancestors.

If you were to visit Scotland you would not fail to visit the lakes and other romantic spots that have been so justly admired.

THE HIGHLANDERS.

## TRAVEL AND ADVENTURE. 113

LOCH KATRINE.

Loch or Lake Katrine, is situated at a distance of little more than twenty-five miles from Stirling, and is remarkable as the scenery of Scott's Lady of the Lake. The lake is approached through a valley surrounded by lofty hills and wild precipices, described by Scott as "a wildering scene of mountains, rocks, and woods, thrown together in disorderly groups."

Its principal charm consists in the singular rugged wildness of its mountain sides and its pretty rocky islets rising to a considerable height out of the water, and tufted over with trees and shrubs.

Near the eastern extremity of the lake there is precisely such an island as that which is described in the poem as the residence of the outlawed Douglas and his family. To fulfil the wishes of the imagination, Lady Willoughby D'Eresby, the owner of the ground, has erected upon the island a sort of tower or cottage, such as that which the said family occupied, in order to carry out the pleasing deception.

The view of the lake on approaching it from the east is rather confined, but from the top of the rocky mountain above the prospect is singularly imposing, and is described by the author of the Lady of the Lake, as follows :

——— "Gleaming with the setting sun,
One burnished sheet of living gold,
Loch Katrine lay beneath him rolled,

> In all her length far winding lay,
> With promontory, creek and bay,
> And islands that empurpled bright,
> Floated amid the livelier light,
> And mountains that like giants stand,
> To sentinel enchanted land,
> High on the south, huge Ben-Venue
> Down on the lake its mosses threw—
> Craigs, knolls and mounds, confusedly hurled,
> The fragments of an earlier world !
> A wildering forest feathered o'er
> His ruined sides and summit hoar;
> While in the north, through middle air,
> Ben-An heaved high his forehead bare."

While we waited one bright July afternoon at the eastern extremity of Loch Katrine, for the steamer that was to take us up the lake, we strolled along the shore, and soon struck into a bridle path which winds its way along the general direction of the northern shore, sometimes coming down to the very verge of the water, and then striking off into some glen densely shaded with the white birch and fir, or over some craggy steep where the toilsome ascent is rewarded with an enchanting view of the lake beneath our feet, and of the solemn hills that perpetually stand as sentinels over it. During our stroll of an hour or two, we were every few moments greeted by the rapturous exclamation of some one of our party, calling our attention to a new discovered beauty of prospect. We surveyed each little recess and promontory with a childish curiosity.

While some gathered treasures for their cabinet, of minerals or herbarium, and some shouted to the top of their voice that they might hear its oft repeated echoes among the hills; others, more poetically inclined, repeated stanzas from the "Lady of the Lake," and endeavored, in what they actually saw, to trace the truthfulness of Sir Walter Scott's scenic delineations. To such the interest of the occasion was not at all diminished by the appearance around a jutting crag, of a young lady on horseback, riding at a rapid pace over the uneven and flinty road. A voice exclaimed, "See the Lady of the Lake." She did not notice us, but rode with an easy grace on an indifferent-looking but easy-paced steed. Her face was flushed from the excitement of the ride; she was plainly but tastefully attired, and her whole bearing was such that it was no unpleasant idea to associate her with the Lady of the Lake. Were we not in a fairy land? and did not the fairy lady preside over the scene that had been made immortal by her presence? From this reverie we were hardly awake, so as to determine whether we were in a land of dreams or of realities, when the lady reined up her steed, and standing awhile to gaze on the laughing lake, she retraced her path, and returning again passed near us. To our salutation she returned a graceful acknowledgment, and disappeared from our view. If "*The* Lady of the Lake" rowed her light canoe more skilfully than our lady of the lake rode her black horse, she is justly entitled to her fame.

We had wandered far, but were not weary, when, in the distance up the lake, we saw the approach of the steamer that was to take us up on its return. We hastened back to the place of embarking, and were soon on board and on our way. The sun was still high in the west, and we would have ample time to complete the tour of the lake before nightfall.

The sail up the lake presents a succession of the most beautiful views that can be imagined. Every hill has its name, and every high rock its story. The eagle circles about the top of Ben-Venue, while the wild goats climb where there is scarcely room for the soles of their feet. Here and there is a sheltered nook where the mountain shepherd has built his stone cottage, but with these exceptions, there are no traces of human abodes. The scene is closed by a west view of the lake, which is ten miles long, and the prospect is bounded by the towering Alps of Arrochar.

Arrived at the west end of the lake, we found that a moorland region, traversed by a rugged path five miles in length, intervened between us and Loch Lomond, on whose shores we wished to spend the night. Shaggy Highland ponies were in attendance, and pony-carts to carry us over. We were soon on our way, some on carts, some on saddles, and some on foot, their baggage being sent forward. We passed a smoky hut in the valley between Loch Katrine and Loch Lomond, in which is exhibited a Spanish musket six feet and a half long, once the property of Rob Roy, whose original residence was in this lone vale. We also saw the hut where it is said that Helen M'Gregor, Rob Roy's wife, was born. Near by this hut were men and women in full Highland costume, at work in a field of hay. After our ride over the moor, which, with the exception of some of the lower valleys, was covered with heather, we arrived at Inversnaid Mill, on Loch Lomond.

A few rods from the hotel a little rivulet comes tumbling down over precipitous rocks and forms a milky cataract, which is the scene of Wordsworth's beautiful poem to the "Highland Girl."

One afternoon, while tarrying at this place, we crossed over the rivulet and strolled up the mountain side; at the distance of about a mile we approached a highland hut, which stood alone and solitary on the bleak eminence that commanded a broad view of Loch Lomond, and of the towering peak of Ben Lomond. Here were no fences to be seen, and nothing to denote the presence of civilization but the low stone walls of the hut, with its thatched roof and two little windows of four panes of seven-by-nine glass, and a little potato patch and cow-house near by.

As we approached, we saw a robust and intelligent looking girl, apparently about twenty years old, standing in the door and watching intently our movements.

Having a curiosity ourselves to see the interior of the lowly dwelling, we entered into conversation with her. She treated us courteously, and replied to all our enquiries with a dignified self-possession, that many a mistress of a proud drawing-room might envy. What, though her feet were bare, and her garments coarse and homespun, they were clean and appropriate to her mode of life. The glow of health was on her cheek, and her whole manner betokened an active, intelligent mind, and a cheerful and buoyant heart.

She pointed out the beauties of the surrounding scenery with an appreciative taste; told us the history of her father's family, and while she was entertaining us, her father, an old man of more than seventy years, approached from his day's toil with a scythe on his shoulder, and, with a courteous tip of his hat, joined our circle.

He said his name was McFarland; this, too, was the name of Wordsworth's "Highland Girl," and for aught we knew, she was of the same family. He was born in that hut; his father, and grandfather, and great grandfather, were born and died there. It had been in the family one hundred and twenty-five years, and during that time had not been repaired, except to be thatched anew from time to time; and the furniture had not been changed. He expected himself to die there ere long, and then his son would take it. It belonged to the estate of the Duke of Montrose, as do all the lands for miles about there. They paid an annual rent of five pounds for the cottage and potato-patch, and pasturage and hay for the cow.

We were kindly invited to go into the cottage and drink a glass of milk. We gladly accepted the invitation, for we were curious to see the interior. There were two rooms, separated by a partial partition, a fire of turf was burning in a rude fire-place, sending out its smoke in every part of the room. Instead of a chimney, there was an opening in the thatch through which part of the smoke escaped. The rafters, and every object in both rooms were literally japanned with crystallized smoke, and shone like glass in the dim light. Instead of floor there was the hard earth, smoothed by the wear of many generations, but still damp and gloomy. The furniture was simple and well worn. The dingy crockery and pewter platters adorned a "dresser" in the corner.

By the fireside, with her knitting in hand, sat the old lady, who for fifty years had been the companion of her husband in that lowly hut, and who was full of cheerfulness and good humor. She read to us from her Gallic Bible and Psalm book, and

LAKE AWE.

told stories in her broad Scotch till the smoky roof resounded with our laughter.

Away over the loche, ten miles distant, they attend church on the Sabbath. To us it would seem that their home-comforts must be few. Their dwelling is a fair sample of many Highland cottages which we afterwards entered. Luxuries the Highlanders have none, and even comforts are few, yet they are content with their lot, and are a cheerful, intelligent, and worthy people, affectionate in their families, loyal to their Queen, and true to their Church.

Loche Awe is another of the celebrated lakes. The cut herewith exhibits a distant view of it, but no description or representation can give any adequate idea of the enchanting reality; we can only hope that our readers will some day have the pleasure of beholding with their own eyes these scenes so full of grandeur, and so suggestive of poetic emotions. But if this privilege is denied them, perhaps they will find in our own country scenes of grandeur and of novel beauty that are not deficient in any thing, unless it be in classic or historic association. The northern part of New Hampshire and Vermont, the western part of Massachusetts, and portions of New York and Pennsylvania, present specimens of varied and romantic scenery that are justly admired, and that need only the associations of historic legends to make them renowned as any spot that is frequented by the sight-seers of the old world.

To the west of Scotland there is a cluster of islands with bleak and rugged surface, known as the Western Islands. They are inhabited by a poor class of peasants who obtain a precarious subsistence from the scanty soil and the sea.

ISLE OF STAFFA.

In this group is the island of *Staffa*, famous for its basaltic cavern called Fingal's Cave.

This cave opens from the sea, and is about 42 feet wide, 66 feet high, and 227 feet deep. The sides are formed of columnar rock, and as the sea never ebbs entirely out, the floor of this beautiful cave is the clear green water, which reflects from its clear bottom the varying shades of the rocks, and produces a beautiful effect.

Imagine yourself sailing into this immense cave, that seems like a pile of masonry built by giants, and now going to decay. It is one of the most impressive and interesting objects to be met with in Scotland.

TRAVEL AND ADVENTURE.    .125

## ELSIE'S SUMMER ADVENTURES.

THE SAILING PARTY.

L IZZIE MORTON was a room-mate of Elsie's at boarding-school. She loves our darling cousin dearly, and though she is much the older, likes to have Elsie always with her. She has invited her many times, but this summer she came herself to see us all, and begged Uncle Hiram to spare Elsie for a little while to go home with her. Her sweet voice and winning ways were powerful charms, and she bore our little cousin off in triumph.

The journey was a long one, and Elsie was half asleep, on the evening of the second day, when Lizzie roused her, exclaiming, "Elsie, Elsie! get your bag ready—here we are, just stopping at the last station, and I'm sure I see brother Charles on the platform!"

Just then the cars stopped, and a young man, whom Lizzie called Charles, came in and welcomed her home.

"Is this your friend Elsie?" asked he, kindly shaking the little girl's hand. "I am very glad you were at last successful, and have brought her with you. We'll have fine times together I promise you, Miss Elsie."

All this time he had been taking up the shawls, baskets, and bags; and now giving his hand to Elsie, he led her out of the car, saying, "Lizzie knows the way, so you are my charge."

When fairly seated in the carriage, Elsie laid her head wearily back, and while the brother and sister talked, she watched the long rows of lights in the streets, and the brilliantly illuminated shop-windows. Charles caught her in his arms, when the carriage stopped, and carried her up the long pathway to the house, where Mrs. Morton was waiting upon the steps. "Here, mother, is Lizzie's Elsie, tired as she can be," he exclaimed, and putting her gently down, ran back for the bags, etc. Elsie did not know just what to do at this unceremonious treatment. She had always seemed older than she was, and her quiet, lady-like manner led people to treat her not quite like a child. It was a long time since any one but Harry, or Uncle Hiram, would have thought of running off with her in his arms. She had not much time for such thoughts, for in a moment Lizzie came running up the steps. "Why, Elsie," she cried, "Charley spirited you off before I had time to think. You'll have to get used to his queer, quick ways, and then you'll love him dearly."

"Will she, indeed?" said Charley, coming behind his sister and stopping her with a kiss. "You had better not stay here to discuss brother Charley, but go in and rest, get some tea, and go to bed. It will require at least a day to canvass my merits."

Elsie was quite as tired as Charley supposed, and fell asleep almost as soon as her head touched the pillow. When she awoke the next morning, the sun was shining brightly into her window. She sprang up immediately, and began to dress. In a moment the door opened, and Lizzie looked in. "I thought I heard you moving," she said. "I have just finished dressing myself."

"But it's *very* late, Lizzie, is it not?" said Elsie. "Why did you let me sleep so long?"

"What a rueful face, Elsie!" cried Lizzie, laughing. "I should think you imagined yourself at boarding-school again, trembling for fear of that six o'clock bell."

"Oh, no, Lizzie," exclaimed Elsie; "that's impossible in this very pretty room."

"It isn't much like the uncarpeted floors and bare rooms we've been used to, is it?" said Lizzie. "This was sister Fanny's room before she was married, and mine is just opposite, and our sitting-room is between them. Oh, such a comfort as that room is! We shall have such quiet times there!"

"But has not the breakfast bell rung?" asked Elsie.

"Yes, indeed, long ago; but I arranged that with mother last night. We are to have breakfast together, whenever we want it, to-day. I knew we should be too sleepy to be punctual."

Mr. Morton's house overlooked the bay, while far, far away one could see the blue ocean. The busy town streets, with their rows of shops, the wharves, the ships, and even the more quiet avenues, with their stately houses, were all new to Elsie. She could amuse herself for hours, seated in the deep window-seat of Lizzie's sitting-room, watching the boats skimming hither and thither over the bright waters of the bay, or counting the white sails in the distance, as the vessels entered or went out of the harbor.

She was not left much to herself, however. Lizzie had numerous friends, who seemed to think that no pic-nic, sail, or party of any kind could be had without her; and Elsie was always her companion.

"Girls," said Arthur one evening at tea, "'tis proposed to go on an island party to-morrow, to one of the outside islands—Kanadeck, I believe—will you go?"

"I had heard nothing about it," said Lizzie. "'Tis rather short notice."

"Oh, 'tis the young men's plan. They are coming round to invite every one in form this evening. We have been making all arrangements this afternoon. It was not thought of till this morning."

"Is Charley going?" asked Mrs. Morton. "I am always afraid of these excursions on the water. But if he goes, I shall feel more like trusting Lizzie and Elsie, he knows so well all the danger, and has so much skill in such matters."

"Here he comes," said Arthur, as Charles' light, quick step was heard. "Of course he is going. Who ever heard of his staying away from any such affair."

Charles was going, of course. He was on the

committee of invitation, and could scarcely stay a moment, having quite a large list to invite. He only came home to tell Elsie, that he should insist on her going, and claimed her as his special charge.

"Well, Charley has settled the matter, I see," said Mrs. Morton, as he went out. "I hope the plan is, to be at home early."

"Oh, mother, you are always so afraid of the water! Just think how many excursions we have taken, and never had the least mishap," said Lizzie.

"Yes, but you stay out so late that I am always anxious."

"I wish I could promise you that this party would be an improvement in that respect, mother," said Arthur; "but the very charm of the thing is, that we are to sail home by moonlight."

"I always hate to go on such parties, and feel that you are in constant anxiety, mother," said Lizzie. "Perhaps we had better give this up."

"No, indeed, Lizzie," said Mrs. Morton. "I see Elsie's face grow grave at the very thought. No doubt you will return as safely as before. It is a constant fear of mine, and you would never go, if you wait for me to feel easy about it."

So it was settled that they should go. Lizzie and Elsie went off to prepare their island attire—for they were to start early in the morning—and Arthur remembered that he still had some arrangements to make, being one of the committee on refreshments.

The sun rose bright and beautiful. Lizzie and Elsie were ready in good season. The boats were to start from a private pier, in the upper part of the town, quite near Mr. Morton's, so that most of the party could easily walk to it.

The pier presented a busy, gay scene as they approached. Several boats were in waiting; some fifty or sixty gentlemen and ladies were gathered in groups on the shore. Such an array of shawls, baskets, hampers, and eatables of all sorts, in every imaginable shape, were never seen before.

It took some time to load the boats, with passengers and freight in due proportion. At length all was done, and the last boat left the pier under the guidance of Charles Morton.

It was quite a mixed company. A very few were young as Elsie; for some whole families, father, mother, and children were there—so that every one had choice of companions.

The sail was delightful. The bay was smooth as glass, and when they reached the islands that skirted it, and wound in and out between them, the scene was varied and charming. Sometimes the boats were near enough to each other for conversation, and sometimes the foremost ones would disappear behind a jutting point, and be lost entirely to sight. At last the island of their destination appeared in view, and beyond, the broad, unbroken ocean.

A difficulty now arose. The water near the shore was too shallow for the boats to approach, and there was no place where the party could land without running the risk of a wetting.

DIAMOND COVE.

"There is 'Diamond Cove' on the other side of this island," said Charley Morton. "I propose we try there, perhaps we can get nearer the shore."

No sooner said than done, and every voice was raised in exclamations of delight, as rounding the weather-beaten cliffs of "White Head" they shot into the "cove." The water, clear as crystal, revealed every treasure of its glassy depths, and the pebbles on the bottom glittered like diamonds. Two high, rocky headlands guarded the entrance to the bay, while within the green shores sloped gradually downward to a white sandy beach.

But amid all these beauties, the attention of all the party was fixed on the distant shore. The woods seemed alive with wild, fantastic figures, dancing, running, leaping, screaming, making the old woods ring with their shouts. It was an Indian encampment.

"I declare," exclaimed Arthur Morton, "the Indians are beforehand with us! How long do you think they have been here, Charley?"

"Not long; for I was here last week," answered his brother. "They have chosen a beautiful place for their summer home, and I think we shall have to make them useful."

So saying, he gave a shrill whistle, and with a motion of his hand signified to the Indians that he wished their help in getting on shore.

At the first appearance of the boats the revelry on shore had ceased. The women and children had disappeared in the deeper shade of the woods, while many of the men were watching the approach of the new comers.

At Charley's signal, two stalwart, fierce-looking men hastened to the shore, each with a canoe on

his head, which he launched and paddled to the
boats. As they drew near, Charles whispered to
the company that he knew the foremost man, as
chieftain of a tribe which often made the islands
their summer home, and enjoined on all to treat
him with respect.

Though half afraid, Elsie could not help watching
the chief with the greatest interest. He was a

noble Indian. A blanket of various colors hung over one shoulder—the other, with his breast being bare, and ornamented with wampum strings, a huge steel plate, like a buckler, and many little charms. His beaded belt and gaudy moccasins, with the single lock of hair on the top of his head, woven with a few showy feathers into a tuft five or six inches high, distinguished him from the rest of the tribe.

"Ah! Miannotto," said Charles Morton, "we are in trouble; can you land us on shore?"

"Ugh," replied the Indian, "me take squaw safe."

Now as these canoes are light as cork and very easily upset, it requires great skill to manage them, and perfect quietness on the part of the passengers. The ladies were about to shrink from trusting themselves in the frail boat alone; but Charles courteously accepted the kind offer of the Indian, and immediately proposed that Lizzie should go first with her brother Arthur.

"No, no," replied Miannotto, "squaw first;" and motioning Arthur back, signed to Elsie to take her place by Lizzie; then, telling them to be still, very still in the bottom of the canoe, he pushed off to the shore, and in a moment the two girls were standing alone on the beach. The other canoe soon brought them company; but not one man would the Indians take, until all the ladies were landed. This was Indian gallantry.

Besides the two Indians who thus assisted our party, not one of the tribe, male or female, came down to the shore to meet them.

As many of the party had never seen an encampment before, the first thing was to pay a visit to the wigwams. Charles took Elsie by the hand, and then, offering his arm to Lizzie, led them round the encampment. On a fallen tree near by, sat two women, one a very beautiful girl about sixteen. She said her name was Margaret. A white lady, some years before, had visited the tribe, and given her many presents, and this name. Her Indian name was Netoka. She was busily working a basket of porcupine quills. Elsie lost all fear in the presence of this gentle girl, and seating herself beside her, tried to learn how the work was done, which pleased Netoka so much that she gave Elsie a little box which she had just finished, while Charles engaged to buy the basket for his mother, as soon as it was ready.

At length all the party, who were strolling in separate groups over the island, were reminded, by a long bugle note, that dinner-time had arrived. Preparations had been made for a sumptuous repast. A large rock, flat and smooth, served for a table, whereon appeared a rich variety of inviting things. In the centre was the indispensable chowder, made of fish just caught from the rocks, and cooked on the spot. There were not half plates enough, to be sure, but their place was well supplied by clam-shells, large leaves, or pieces of slaty rock.

It was a merry scene and a joyous feast. There had been enough of exertion during the day to insure a good appetite to all, and they did ample justice to the off-hand cookery. After dinner, while some were appointed to dispose of the fragments, and pack the baskets, others threw themselves on the grass in little groups, telling stories, singing songs, and forgetting everything else in the pleasure of the moment.

Suddenly they were startled by a loud peal of thunder. "We shall have a storm," cried one; "can we get home first?"

"No, indeed," said Charles Morton, the sailor of the party; "don't you see it coming?" and he pointed to the black cloud which was hurrying toward them.

"Perhaps it will be only a squall, and if we have bright moonlight after it, we shall not mind," said one.

"But how escape drenching here?" asked another.

"Go back to the Indians; and the ladies, at least, can be sheltered in the wigwams, or under the canoes," was Arthur's proposition.

Instantly every one was on the move. The Indians received this sudden addition to their household as silently and indifferently as they did every thing else ; but they quietly gave shelter to every one, and that was all that was asked.

The storm passed without doing any harm to the party on the island, but it was followed by a dense fog, so common to the coast, and it was evidently impossible to attempt going home while that lasted.

"What shall be done?" asked Charles Morton, when he had assembled the whole company for a consultation. "I am fairly puzzled. This is more than I bargained for—to provide house and home for so many."

"What has become of old Joe Barker's fishing boat?" asked his brother; "was it on this island?"

"I believe it was," said Charles; "we must explore the whole island, and see what we can find."

"While you are looking up huts, we will go out to the boats and bring back the sails, and such other things as we need; perhaps we can manage to make a hut for ourselves."

Charles soon returned. He had found the hut in pretty good preservation, and was sure that the girls could make it quite comfortable with shawls and cloaks, for our island parties are always prepared for a change of weather. He piloted the party through the woods to the old hut. It was of the rudest kind, but still a most welcome shelter. A large fire was burning in front of the door, by which the new quarters were soon made dry and cheerful. Those who could not find room in the hut spread a large sail on the ground, and hung another over it for a roof. Shawls pinned to the sides, served for walls, and the tent was complete.

THE SAFE RETURN.

Thus snugly quartered, Lizzie proposed that the

ladies should prepare tea. The remains of the dinner were unpacked, put in fine order, and, in the absence of tables and chairs, passed round to the party, all of whom were determined to make the most of their novel and amusing predicament.

There was very little sleeping, of course, that night. The watch-fire burned brightly, and stories, songs, and pleasant talk filled up the swift hours till the dawn.

Meanwhile, all was anxiety in the town. Every one knew that it was impossible to navigate the narrow, crooked passes among the islands in such a fog. Had the party started before the fog appeared? that was the question. Poor Mrs. Morton could not sleep for anxiety, and the moment it was light she was up watching the bay and the distant islands. At length eager to catch the first glimpse of the returning party, and assure themselves of their safety, she and her husband, with Mr. and Mrs. Burton, drove over to the Cape. Here, on the high cliffs, they had a full view of bay and islands. They had not been there long ere the boats appeared, one after the other, skimming swiftly over the waves. Mr. Morton raised his handkerchief on his cane, and waved it toward the boats. The signal was seen and answered by a loud cheer; and then, clambering down the rocks the watchers drove rapidly homeward.

"There is no harm done, only a little famine in

the camp," was Charles Morton's only answer to the many inquiries put to him. "Bring on the breakfast, and please remember hungry men are not very amiable."

No one suffered from the unusual exposure ; but whenever an island party is proposed, some one is sure to say, " Yes, yes, if we only could stay all night, and be sure to have as pleasant a time as at Diamond Cove."

Elsie thinks this one of the most remarkable adventures of her summer's visit, and I hope the Merry family will be as much interested in reading it, as we all were when she told it to us.

## ADVENTURE OF A DOG.

"JERRY."

"JERRY" is a general favorite in and around his native city, Nevada, and although he signifies his appreciation of pats or words of kindness by a gentle wagging of his tail, he neither follows nor obeys any one but his master.

The first time we saw him, Mr. Dawley requested him to shut the door—which was wide open, and against the wall—when he immediately put his nose behind it, and closed it; but as it did not "catch," he raised upon his hind legs, and threw the whole weight of his body against it, and thus effectually shut it.

"Go, sit down there, Jerry," said his master; and he immediately went to the spot indicated and sat down. "Sit up, Jerry," and up he sat. "Stand up, Jerry, and come to me;" and what appeared to us as very singular, he arose from his sitting posture and stood erect upon his hind feet, and then walked in an erect position to his master.

"Lie down and die, Jerry." He immediately lay down at his master's feet, and closed his eyes, and appeared like one dead; when Mr. D. slipped his right hand under one side, and his left under the other, about his middle, as he lay upon the floor, to lift him up; and the dog did not move a muscle or a limb, but his body hung down as helplessly as though he were really dead.

"Up, Jerry," and he soon let us know that he was worth a dozen dead dogs. "Take a chair, Jerry," and he was soon seated in the only vacant chair in the room. "Now, wink one eye, Jerry," and one eye was accordingly "winked" without ceremony. Jerry, however, did not enlighten us upon the subject of having practiced this ungentlemanly habit, when passing some of his canine lady friends in the public streets! but perhaps thinking that this might be used to criminate himself, he only wagged his tail by way of answer, which simply meant either yes or no—just as we pleased—to our interrogations.

He used to be very fond of these amusements, until he saw a little quarrelsome dog, against whom he had taken a dislike, practicing the same tricks, when he evidently became disgusted, and very reluctantly obeyed his master for some time afterward.

Mr. Dawley is the owner of some mining claims on Wet Hill, and resides near them; and as they are worked both day and night, whenever the time arrives to "change the watch," he will say to the dog, "Jerry, go and call Ben" (or any one else, as the case may be, for he knows every one of their names distinctly,) when he immediately goes to the cabin door of the man wanted, which is left a little ajar, opens it, and commences pulling off the bedclothing; and if this does not awake the sleeper, he jumps upon the bed and barks, until he succeeds in his undertaking.

If a candle goes out, in the tunnel, it is placed in his mouth, as shown in the engraving, and he goes to the man named, to get it re-lighted.

About a year ago, when they were running their tunnel, he would lie down at the entrance, and allow no stranger to enter, without the consent of his master; but when told by him that it was all right, he not only appeared pleased, but barked at a candle that was sticking in the side of the tunnel, when his master lighted it, placed it in his mouth, and said to him, "Show this gentleman the diggings, Jerry," and he directly started, with his lighted candle, and led the way into every drift.

There is a shaft to the diggings, something over two hundred feet in depth, and should he want to go down at any time, which he often does, he goes to the top, and, on finding the dirt bucket up, will without hesitation jump in, entirely of his own accord, and descend to the bottom.

Mr. Chambers, an inmate of the cabin in which Jerry was raised, and who knew him from a pup, entered for the purpose of getting a coat, but when he took hold of it, the dog began to growl, and would not permit him to take it out, in the absence of his master, and he had, after considerable coaxing, to leave without it. He allows the washerman to enter the cabin on a Saturday, with the clean clothes, but as the man takes one chair, he immediately takes another chair opposite, and sits watching him until his master enters; nor will he by any means allow him to take away again, even the clothes he brought with him.

If men are sitting and conversing in the cabin, he will take a chair with the rest, and, what is somewhat remarkable, he always turns his head, and keeps looking at the one who is speaking, as though paying the utmost attention. We might suggest an imitation of Jerry's good manners to older heads than his, with much less sense within them—especially when present in a church or lecture room—but we forbear, except to ask, that whenever they become listless at such times and in such places, they always think of " Jerry !"

Jerry, too, is "general carrier" for his master, and goes to town each morning for the daily papers. On one occasion he was carrying home some meat, when a much larger dog than he sallied out upon him, to try to steal it from him, but he took no notice of him, except to keep his tail near the enemy, and his head (with the meat) as far away as possible; but when the large dog supposed Jerry to be somewhat off his guard, he made a sudden though unsuccessful spring at the meat, when Jerry, as if *struck* with a new idea, immediately started home as fast as possible ; and after he had deposited it safely in the cabin, he returned to town, and gave his thieving-disposed brother a good sound whipping ; now, the enemy has a great preference for the opposite side of the street whenever he sees Jerry coming up.

Whenever his master goes to town, the dog stands watching him at the door, and never attempts to accompany him, without a look or a nod of acquiescence. If Mr. D. purchases a pair of pants, or gloves, or anything else, immediately after arriving in town, he will say to him, "Jerry, you see these are mine," and place them on one side ; and after remaining an hour or two in town, and going to different places—sometimes to the theater—he says, " Jerry, I guess I'll go home now," when the dog starts off directly for the parcel left, and appears with it in his mouth, wagging his tail, as much as to say : "Here we are—is this right ?" He always remembers very correctly where it was left for him.

About noon, on Saturday last, his master said to him : "Jerry, I don't want you to go with me this afternoon, as Mrs. Houston wishes you to go to town with her ;" when he lay quietly down, and never attempted to move, as he generally does, to accompany his master to his work. He waited very patiently until Mrs. H. was putting on her bonnet, when, taking up a small parcel which he had seen her place upon a chair, he waited with it in his mouth until she was ready to go, and then followed her down. When in town, Mrs. H. bought a bonnet box, about fifteen inches square, with a handle on top, and said to him : "Jerry, I want that carried home," when he took the handle in his mouth, to try to carry it ; but as it extended up to his breast, and prevented his taking his usual step, he set it down again, when she said : " Never mind, Jerry, if that is too much for you, I will send for it ;" he immediately took it up, and although he could not lift it more than two inches from the ground, he carried it all the way home for her.

He will lift at a sack of gold dust until his hind feet are both several inches from the floor. If sent to a store across the street for a jug of liquor, and he can not carry it, he will be sure to drag it over —if at all possible—and never mistakes an empty one for a full one. When his master asks him to fetch his socks, or his boots, or his hat, or coat, or anything else, he never gets the wrong article, as he has a good memory to remember the names of everything told him.

To see what he would do, several men, with his master's consent, tied a string and pan to his tail, but instead of running off as most dogs would, he turned and bit the string in two; then took hold of the string and dragged the pan along. He will go up and down a ladder by himself. If several men are in the cabin, and his master on going out should tell him not to leave it, all of them combined would not be able to coax him out.

He is very fond of music, and will walk about for hours, wagging his tail, whenever Mr. Curtis (a miner living in the same cabin) plays upon the banjo; and sometimes he would run around, catching at his tail, and barking when the music ceased.

"Jerry" has more friends than any man in town, as everybody likes him for his good-natured eccentricities, intelligence, and amusing performances.

He sleeps at night in an arm-chair near his master's head, and seems to love and watch over him with the utmost fondness and solicitude. If, however, the blanket upon which he sleeps is thrown carelessly into the chair at night, or is not perfectly straight and smooth, he will not attempt to occupy it until it is made all right.

Many, very many other performances of interest could be related, such as picking up money and carrying it to his master; catching paper in his mouth if placed upon his nose; taking off his own collar; unfastening ropes with his teeth; jumping over chairs; carrying away his master's gloves on Saturday night and returning them on Monday morning; standing in any position told him; fetching anything asked for, etc., etc., almost *ad infinitum*. But we think that we have said sufficient to prove that Jerry is an intelligent dog; and yet some persons, with more vanity than veneration, will persist in believing that God's works are not as perfect and as beautiful as they are, by asserting that "dogs have no souls," while they admit them to possess all the attributes of intelligence—except in the same degree—as those found in men; and we must say that we have witnessed more true nobility of *mind* in some dogs than we have in *some* men.

## MERRY'S BOOK OF

### THE GLADIATORS.

**G**LADIATORS were combatants who fought at the public games in Rome, for the entertainment of the spectators. They were at first prisoners, slaves, or condemned criminals, but afterwards freemen fought in the arena, either for hire or from choice. The regular gladiators were instructed in schools intended for this purpose. Overseers of this school purchased the gladiators and maintained them. They were hired of him by those who wished to exhibit games to the people. The games were commenced by a *prælusio*, in which they fought with weapons of wood, till, upon a signal, they assumed their arms, and began in earnest to fight in pairs. In case the vanquished was not killed in the combat, his fate was decided by the people. If they decreed his death, the thumb was held up in the air; the opposite motion was a signal to save him. In general, the doomed gladiator suffered death with wonderful firmness, and often heroically bared his bosom to the death blow. If he wished to appeal to the people, he raised his hand. When a gladiator was killed in the arena, attendants appointed for the purpose, dragged the body with iron hooks into a room prepared for this use. The victors received a branch of palm or a palm garland. They were often released from further servitude, and as a badge of freedom, received a wooden sword.

We can readily conceive that when brought to the dread conflict in which the alternative before them was an ignominious slaughter or a life of freedom, they would fight with a desperate courage, and perform almost superhuman feats of strength and skill. They often were captives, that by the chances of war had been torn from home and friends and country, and all that is dear in life, and on the fate of this one struggle depended all of hope and happiness that this world held out to them.

But it not unfrequently happened that captives from the same country—friends, relations, brothers—by the merciless decree of their cruel captors, were arrayed in this death struggle against each other. Those who had been companions in youth, companions in war, and in defeat, who had lived and loved together, were doomed to fight against each other, to gratify the imperious and cruel taste of spectators more degraded and far more depraved than the poor slaves that were sacrificed to gratify their morbid desires.

The history of humanity impresses us with this truth, that the human character is made up of strange contrasts and inconsistencies. It seems strange, and almost incredible to us, that a people like the Romans, so cultivated in their literature, and so far advanced in civilization, and so exalted in many of their attributes, should yet cherish the sanguinary and cruel spirit that could find amusement and pleasure in the barbarities of a gladiatorial struggle, should delight in the flow of human blood, and in the merciless sacrifice of one who fought for dear life, and perhaps for wife, and home and children, yet such is the fact. Gladiatorial combats were reserved for feast-days and occasions of special joy. They were patronized and paid for by the opulent and titled—the very elite of the realm. Handsome ladies, arrayed in their costly attires, and decked with jewels of untold wealth, found a pleasure in the excitements of the death struggle between the poor combatants. Were these persons devoid of sensibility? No; there were many of them endowed with noble natures. They were kind and sympathizing; they loved as mothers and sisters. Then how can we account for this strange, this cruel taste? It was the effect of education. Many enormities were tolerated in past ages, which are now no more. We do not believe the world is growing worse, but better; and we have reason to be grateful that we live in these later times.

## THE FOUR HENRYS.

ONE night when the rain fell in torrents, an old woman, renowned for sorcery, who lived in a poor cabin in the forest of Saint Germain, heard a knocking at the door. She opened it, and beheld a cavalier, who entreated her hospitality. She put his horse in the barn and bade him enter. By the light of a smoking lamp she saw that he was a young nobleman. His figure betrayed his youth, and his dress his rank. The old woman kindled a fire, and inquired whether he wished anything to eat. A stomach sixteen years old is like a heart of the same age, very greedy, and little squeamish. The young man eagerly accepted her offer. A scrap of cheese and a morsel of black bread came out of the trough—it was the old woman's entire store.

"I have nothing more," said she to the young nobleman. "There is all that the tithes, the rents, and the salt tax, leave me to offer to poor travelers; not counting that the peasants in the neighborhood say I am a sorceress and in league with the devil, that they may steal the produce of my poor field with a clear conscience."

"Pardieu!" said the noble, "if ever I become king of France, I will suppress the taxes, and instruct the people."

"May God hear you," said the dame.

As she spoke, the nobleman approached the table to partake of the slender fare, but at the same moment a new knocking at the door interrupted him. The old woman opened it and saw another cavalier, drenched with the rain, who entreated for admission. It was granted him, and, having entered, he showed himself to be a young man of high rank.

"Is it you, Henry?" said the first.

"Yes, Henry," replied the other.

Both were named Henry. The old woman learned from their conversation that they belonged to a large hunting party, led by King Charles IX., which the storm had dispersed.

"Old woman," said the newcomer, "have you nothing else to give us?"

"Nothing," replied she.

"Then," said he, "we will divide what is before us."

The first Henry made a wry face, but observing the resolute eye and vigorous bearing of the second Henry, he said in a vexed tone,

"Divide then!"

A thought occurred as he said this, which he did not express.

"Share with him lest he take the whole."

They sat opposite each other, and one of them had already cut the bread with his dagger, when a third knock was heard at the door. The meeting was singular; 'twas another nobleman, another young man, another Henry. The old woman beheld them with astonishment. The first wished to hide the bread and cheese, the second replaced them on the table, and laid his sword by their side.

The third Henry smiled.

"You don't wish to give me any of your supper then?" said he; "I can wait, I have a good stomach."

"The supper," said the first Henry, "belongs by right to the first comer."

"The supper," said the second, "belongs to him who can best defend it."

The third Henry colored with anger, and said fiercely:

"Perhaps it belongs to him who best obtains it."

Scarcely were these words uttered, when the first Henry drew his dagger, and the others their swords. As they were about coming to blows, a fourth knock was heard, a fourth young man, a fourth nobleman, a fourth Henry appeared. At the sight of the naked swords, he drew his own, placed himself on the weaker side, and fought rashly.

The old woman, terrified, hid herself, and the swords went clashing and shattering everything that met them in the way. The lamp fell down, went out, and they struck in the dark. The clash of steel lasted for some time, then gradually it grew fainter, and at last suddenly ceased.

Then the old woman ventured out of her hiding-place, relit the lamp, and found the four young men stretched out on the earth, each with a wound. She examined them; fatigue, rather than the loss of blood, had overthrown them. They raised themselves one after the other, and ashamed of what had happened, they laughed and said:

"Come, let us sup peaceably and without any more discord."

But when they looked for the supper, it was on the ground, trampled under foot, and soiled with blood. Slight as it was they regretted it. On the other hand, the cabin was torn down, and the old woman, seated in a corner, fixed her tawny eyes on the four young men.

"Why do you look at us?" said the first Henry, disturbed by her unfaltering gaze.

"I see your destinies written on your foreheads," replied the old woman. The second Henry could hardly retain his self-possession. The last two began to laugh. The old woman continued:

" As you all four have been united in this cabin, you will all four be united in the same destiny. As you have trampled under foot and soiled with blood the bread which hospitality has offered you, so shall you trample under foot and soil with blood the power which you would share. As you have spoiled and impoverished this cottage, you will spoil and impoverish France. As you have all four been wounded in the dark, you will all four perish by treachery and a violent death."

The four noblemen could not forbear laughing at the old woman's prediction.

These four noblemen, were the four heroes of the League, two as its chiefs, two as its enemies.

Henry de Condé, poisoned by his servants.

Henry de Guise, assassinated by the Quarante-cinq.

Henry de Valois, (Henry III.) assassinated by Jacques Clement.

Henry de Bourbon, (Henry IV.) assassinated by Ravaillac.

## SPECTRE OF THE BROCKEN.

PETER Peterson, and his brother Hans, lived in a little village in Hanover, just at the foot of the highest of the Hartz Mountains, the celebrated Brocken. It was a wild, beautiful country. The steep, rocky mountains looked as if resolved that no human foot should climb them ; the gloomy forest-trees stood close together, like ranks of soldiers, ready to repel any invasion of their territory ; and the turbulent streams leaped down precipices, and forced their way through deep caverns, as if to defy any attempt to cross them. Yet people did live at the foot of these mountains, their cattle grazed on the patches of open pasturage, and sometimes forced themselves a short distance into the thick, frowning forests, and drank of the rushing streams. Sometimes, too, they would stray so far in these wilds that the poor peasants would have to follow them and drive them home ; but they did so, trembling with fear, for they well knew that if these places were rough and inaccessible to man, they were the favorite haunts of the wild man of the forest. Did not the weird huntsman sound his horn and dash through those passes in the night ? and when the wind blew and the storm raged, had not the hosts of darkness been heard hurrying on their spectral steeds to their rendezvous ?

SPECTRE OF THE BROCKEN.

Peter and Hans had heard all these things, and believed them, too. Had not their grandmother told them, over and over again, how the spirits of the air, spirits of the earth, and spirits of the water reveled in those very mountains, woods, and streams, so near and yet so terrible to them?

Peter and Hans were both brave lads, not more inclined to superstition than most lads of their age. They only believed and trembled at what all the world around them believed and trembled at.

But Peter and Hans were curious, too, and they were not cowards either; so that their curiosity would often get the better of their prudence, and they would venture on some part of the forbidden, or enchanted ground.

One day, as they were driving homeward the flock they had been watching, Peter exclaimed, "Look! Hans, see how bright the sun shines on the top of the Brocken. Do you suppose the old fellow up there sees it, or is it too bright for his eyes?"

"Perhaps it is," said Hans. "You know he was never seen, except about sunrise, so I think he must walk about at night, and go to bed in the daytime."

"So he says 'good night' to the sun, when he's getting up. I wonder how he can keep his eyes open, when the great sun is wide awake, and sends such a flood of light down on the earth," said Peter.

"It could not do us any harm to look at that old fellow some morning at sunrise," said Hans. "I declare I am tired of hearing about these folk, and never seeing them."

"It would only do you harm if they should see you," replied Peter.

"I don't mean that they shall see me," answered Hans, "that is, not near enough to touch me. Besides, I only intend to see the specter up here on the Brocken, and that I can do by climbing that hill, yonder."

"Well, you have some spirit in you, after all, Hans, and I have a mind to go with you. Two are better than one," cried Peter.

"Yes, two are better than one," said Hans, slowly.

"I don't know," said Peter; "we will fix a time by-and-by."

"No, indeed," exclaimed Hans; "wait till your courage oozes away, or somebody hears us talking of it, and stops us. *I* shall go to-morrow."

The boys had now reached home. They did not venture to say anything more on the subject, lest their careful mother should thwart their plan.

Early the next morning the boys were up. It was their duty daily. Every one in the cottage rose early. This morning, at least, there was no lingering. They drove their flock to the foot of the mountain, and then, with no time to lose, began swiftly to ascend it. When they reached the top, there, full before them, stood the Brocken. The sun's rays had just touched the very summit with a faint tinge of rose color. Not a cloud was to be seen, not a mist to intercept their view; but the specter was not there.

"He never does come out in a clear day," said Hans, pettishly.

"They say he always manages to cover himself with mist and clouds, so you don't see him so plainly as we could if we were there now. What a grand view we could have at him if he only would come out of his hiding-place!"

The next morning the boys ascended the mountain again. Hans was a little in advance, and as he turned a projecting rock, and stood on the very topmost point, the Brocken, vailed in light vapor, was before him, and there, terrible in its shadowy vastness, stood the gigantic form of the specter. Hans stood a moment, trembling, and then, recovering his courage, turned back to call his brother. "He is there, and I have seen him, Peter," he whispered.

Peter shrank back.

"Oh, you need not be afraid," said Hans; "he did not notice me nor harm me. There are some dreadful chasms and precipices between this and the Brocken. Even his giant foot could not step over them."

Thus reassured, Peter came up and looked, but the specter was gone. His strength, too, was gone, and he lay down, panting, while Hans stood by him, looking earnestly at the spot where he had seen the specter. Suddenly he appeared again. Hans did not take off his eyes, but turned toward Peter, and whispered, "He is there again; look!"

Peter, crouching close to the ground, looked up, and saw the awful form, standing motionless, except that the wind blew his long coat's fantastic folds hither and thither.

He seemed looking toward them. At last Hans raised his hand to his cap, fearful that it might be blown off. The specter did the same.

Hans was frightened. The specter certainly noticed them, and had mocked him. What did it mean? Without turning his eyes, he leaned over toward his brother, and whispered, "Peter, do you see that? He saw, and mocked me. He is watching us."

To his horror, the specter also leaned to the ground, as if speaking to some one near him.

"Lift me up," cried Peter; "help me to run away. Let us get away from this place before he springs over to us."

"He can't do that," said Hans, growing brave as he saw his brother's fear; "I will lie down beside you, and see what he will do."

Hans laid down, and to his astonishment, the specter vanished.

"He has only taken some short way hither, or gone, perhaps, to call some other creatures like himself," whispered Peter, in an agony of fear. "Let us go quickly."

Hans trembled too. He was more afraid of the specter invisible than when he saw him on the distant mountains, and knew that they were separated by impassable gulfs. So, giving his hand to Peter, he helped him to rise, shaking in every limb. But instead of running, they stood petrified with fear. The specter too had risen, as if from the earth, dragging with him another figure as large, as terrible in every respect as himself.

Unable to move, the poor boys might have stood there till petrified with fear. But suddenly the sun broke through the clouds, chased away the mists, and shone full and clear on the Brocken and all the neighboring peaks. The specter and his awful companion vanished in the clear sunlight, the boys' courage returned, and soon they were able to return home.

Poor Peter, however, could not soon recover from the shock his nerves had sustained. At length, to explain the singular change in looks and health, Hans was obliged to tell the story of their adventure. It spread through the village; young men and maidens, old men and children, all flocked to Hans to hear his story. All the stories that had ever been told of the "Old Man of the Mountain,"

"The Huntsman of the Hartz," and the "Specter," and hundreds of such personages, were rehearsed over and over again by the grandams. Yet no one dared venture out, except in broad day-light, with every precaution against the evil influence of demons.

It was not until many, many years afterward, that a traveler, wiser than the poor peasants, proved, to his own satisfaction, and theirs too, that the specter was only a reflection of the person who stood on the other mountain, thrown by the sun on the mists of the Brocken.

The relative heights of the two peaks was such, that the first slant rays of the rising sun would glance over the summit of one to that of the other, carrying with them the images of whatever objects were in the way.

Thus the people of the Hartz had for years been afraid of their own shadows, like many wiser people even in this day.

## KING RODERICK AND THE ENCHANTED CAVERN.

SPAIN, during the middle ages, on account probably of its possessing so large a stock of Arabian learning and superstition, was believed to be a favorite residence of magicians. Pope Sylvester, who brought the Arabian manual from Spain into the other parts of Europe, was supposed to have learned in the former country the magic arts for which he was stigmatized by the ignorance of his age. In fact, there were public schools at Toledo, Seville and Salamanca, where magic, or rather the natural sciences which were supposed to contain the mysteries of the magical art, were regularly taught. In Salamanca, the schools were held in a deep cavern, the mouth of which was afterwards walled up by order of Queen Isabella of Castile.

The celebrated magician, Maugis, cousin to Rinaldo of Montalban, called by Ariosto, Malagigi, studied the black art at Toledo. He even held a professor's chair in the necromantic university, which the vulgar believed to have been founded by Hercules, who was taught the magical science by Atlas, along with astronomy and the other liberal arts. Don Roderick, the last of the Gothic Kings of Spain, who lost his life in battle with the Saracen invaders, A. D. 710, is said to have had a remarkable adventure in one of these enchanted caverns near Toledo, which is thus related in a Spanish book, called the true history of the King Don Roderick.

About a mile east of the city of Toledo, among some rocks, was situated an ancient tower of magnificent architecture, though much dilapidated by time, that great destroyer who consumes everything. Twenty or thirty feet below it was a cave with a very narrow entrance, and a gate cut out of the solid rock, lined with a strong covering of iron, and fastened with many locks. Above the gate some Greek letters were engraved, which, although abbreviated, and of doubtful meanings, were thus interpreted according to the exposition of learned men: "The King, who opens this cave, and can discover the wonders, will gain the knowledge of both good and evil things." Many kings desired to know the mystery of this tower, and took great pains to learn how it might be discovered. But when they opened the gate, such a tremendous noise arose in the cavern, that it seemed as if the earth was about to burst asunder. Many persons grew sick with terror, and others dropped down dead.

To guard against these dangers, for it was supposed that a most perilous enchantment was contained within, new locks were put upon the gate, and the entrance was more strongly defended. The belief was, that a king was destined to open it, but that the time had not yet come. At length the King Don Roderick, led on by his evil star and unlucky destiny, opened the tower, and entered the mysterious regions in company with four bold attendants, although they were all agitated with fear. Having proceeded a good way they fled back to the entrance, terrified by a frightful vision which they had beheld.

The king was greatly moved, and ordered many torches to be brought, so contrived that the tempest in the cave could not extinguish them. Then the king entered, not without fear, before all the others. They discovered by degrees a splendid hall, apparently built in a very sumptuous manner. In the centre stood a bronze statue of very ferocious appearance, holding a battle-ax in its hands. With this weapon it struck the floor violently, giving such heavy blows, that the motion of the air caused all the terrible noise which was heard in the cave.

The king, greatly affrighted, began to conjure this terrible visitation, promising that he would return without doing any injury in the cave, after he had obtained a sight of what was contained in it. The statue ceased to strike the floor, and the king, with his followers, somewhat assured and recovering their courage, proceeded into the hall. On the left of the statue they found this description on the wall, "Unfortunate king! thou hast entered here in evil hour." On the right side of the hall these words were inscribed, "By strange nations thou shalt be dispossessed, and thy subjects foully degraded." On the shoulders of the statue other words were written, which said, "I call upon the Arabs!" And upon his breast was written, "I do my office." At the entrance of the hall was placed a round bowl, from which proceeded a loud noise like the fall of water. They found nothing else in the hall, and when the king, sorrowful and greatly affected, had turned round to leave the place, the statue again began to beat the floor with his battle-axe.

After all the company had mutually promised to conceal from the knowledge of others, everything which they had seen, they again closed the tower, and blocked up the gate of the cavern with earth, that no memory might remain in the world of such a portentous and evil-boding prodigy. The ensuing midnight they heard great cries and clamor in the cave, resounding like the noise of battle, and the ground shook with a dreadful roar. The old tower then fell in ruins to the ground with a tremendous crash, causing them unspeakable terror; for the vision, which they had beheld, appeared to them as a dream.

The king afterwards caused wise men to explain what the inscription signified. These persons having consulted together, and studied their meaning, disclosed that the statue of bronze, and the motions which it made with its battle-axe, signified *Time*, and that its office, alluded to in the inscription on its breast, was, that he never rests a single moment. The words on the shoulders, "I call upon the Arabs," they expounded to mean that in time the kingdom of Spain would be conquered by that people. The words upon the left wall signified the destruction of King Roderick, the dreadful calamities which were to fall upon the Spaniards and Goths, and that the unfortunate monarch would be dispossessed of all his dominions. Finally, the letters on the portal indicated that good would betide to the conquerors, and evil to the conquered—of which experience proved the truth.

## THE MOUNTAIN LUTE.

MONT BLANC.

I WILL now give you an account of an adventure which befell me among the mountains of Switzerland.

From the highest summit of those hills that overlook the vale of Lucca on the Savoy, I was contemplating the extended landscape around me. More than half way down the hill, I saw a hamlet, that assured me of a lodging for the night. Thus freed

from inquietude, I allowed my mind to roam at
large in contemplation, and my eye to wander from
one object to another of the spacious view. But
soon the sylvan choristers' last song admonished
me to think of seeking shelter for the night. The
sun, already sunk behind the opposite mountain,
colored with his gold and purple rays the clouds
that seemed to float just above the trees that cover
its summit. I descended slowly; the twilight now
began to veil the horizon with a shade, which by
degrees grew browner, till the empress of night
dispelled the darkness with her silver beams. I
sat down for a moment, to enjoy the picture. Nothing intercepted my view throughout the vast expanse, and I contemplated the infinite extent at
leisure. From the trembling moon, and stars that
twinkled while I gazed upon them, my eye passed
over the calm and spotless azure of the firmament.
The air was fresh, nor did the slightest breeze disturb it. Nature was absorbed in universal silence,
save the low murmur of a stream meandering
through the country at a distance. Stretched upon
the grass, I might perhaps have contemplated till
sunrise; but the music of a lute, made more harmonious by a voice, struck upon my ear, and I felt
the delight of fancying myself suddenly transported
as in a dream to what are called the regions of enchantment. "A lute upon the mountain!" said I,
and turned to that side whence the melody pro-

ceeded, and discovered through the dark verdure of the trees, the white walls and garden paling of a cottage. I approached it and beheld a young peasant with a lute, on which he was playing with exquisite address. A woman standing at his left, kept looking on him with infinite affection. Standing about were many people, all in attitudes of pleasure and attention.

When I first made my appearance, several of the children came to meet me, looked at each other, and said among themselves, "What gentleman is this?" The young musician turned his head, but did not leave off playing. I held out my hand; he gave me his, which I seized with a sort of transport. Every one now rose up and made a circle round us. I informed them, as concisely as I could, of my business in that quarter of the country, and at such a time of night. "We have not an inn for many miles about," remarked the youthful peasant; "we live far from any road; but if you are content to put up with a cottage and poor people, we will do our best to entertain you. You are fatigued, I fancy. Didier, bring a chair. Excuse me, sir; I owe my neighbors the evening entertainment I am now giving them."

I would not take the chair, but laid myself upon the grass, as the rest did. Every one had now resumed his former posture; and the silence I had interrupted took place again.

TRAVEL AND ADVENTURE. 175

THE LUTE PLAYER.

The young man immediately began to play upon his mountain lute; and to sing a favorite ballad, which he did with so much sweetness, that I could see tears stand trembling in the eye of every listener by the time he had repeated the first couplet. After he had finished, the whole company rose up, wiping tears from their eyes. They wished each other a good-night with perfect cordiality. The neighbors with their children went away, and none were left, except an old man upon a seat beside the door, whom till now I had not noticed, the musician, with the woman sitting by him, Didier, the young boy whose name I recollected, and myself.

"Dear sir," said the old man, "you are content, I fancy, with your evening's entertainment? You shall repose in my bed." "No, father," interrupted Didier, who came running from the barn, "I have been spreading me some straw, and it is my bed the gentleman shall lie in, if he pleases." I was forced to promise I would yield to this last offer. Didier, upon this, held out his hand; the old man rested on his shoulder and went in, after wishing me a good-night; we soon followed into the cottage, where, to my astonishment, I saw an air of order and propriety about me. After having made a plentiful, but light repast, upon such fruits as I was told the mountain yielded, Didier led me to a niche in one of the apartments; it was rather narrow, but the bed that filled it was both clean and wholesome. This bed, the little fellow told me, he released with pleasure in my favor. It was not long before I fell into a downy slumber, and my sleeping thoughts were occupied upon the charming objects I had recently witnessed. I did not, all the following day, quit this happy family, and if my fortune should in future permit me, I intend to make a yearly visit to this mountain, for the purpose of revisiting my friends, and filling my heart with those sensations of content and peace which their society and habitation cannot but inspire.

## DUSHMANTA.

HE most powerful of the sovereigns of India, was Dushmanta, and his wealth and magnificence had no bounds. But he was proud and arrogant in his riches, and he shut his heart to the meaner class of his people, and bowed his scepter only to the princes and nobles who stood around his throne.

This conduct sorely grieved an aged Bramin, who had been his teacher in the days of his youth. And he left his hermitage, strewed dust upon his head, and presented himself at the splendid portal of the royal palace.

Here he was observed by the king, who commanded the Bramin to be brought before him.

"Wherefore," he asked, "dost thou appear in the garb of mourning, and why doth dust cover thy venerable head?"

"When I quitted thee," answered the Bramin, "thou wert the wealthiest of all the monarchs of

India, who had ever sat upon the throne of thy fathers. For Brama had blessed thee beyond conception, and joy was in my heart when I left the dwelling of the king, my master. But tidings have reached me in my solitude that all thy wealth has vanished, and that abject poverty is now thy lot."

Dushmanta heard these words with amazement, and smiled. "What fool," he said, "has told thee this falsehood? Behold this palace, the gardens which surround it, and the servants who attend my bidding."

"All this," answered the venerable Bramin, "is but an illusion, which cannot dazzle the truly wise. The sovereign of India has fallen from his high condition into poverty."

Then the king wondered still more at the words of the wise Bramin, and said—"Who then hath witnessed it and told thee, and whose report deserves more credit than the sight of my eyes and the touch of my hands?"

The aged man then lifted up his voice, and said —"The sun, the emblem of truth, beneath the throne of Brama, the clouds above our heads, and the fruit tree before my hut, announce and attest to me thy poverty."

Dushmanta was silent, while the old man proceeded thus—"That Brama hath endowed the luminary of day with inexhaustible light and heat, I am assured by its beams, which, from its rising to its setting, are poured upon every blade of grass, upon my cottage as upon thy palace, and which are reflected in every dew-drop as in the vast ocean. The cloud, when fraught with rain, moves over hill and dale, and alike moistens with its abundance the parched clod and the thirsty mountain. The fruit tree bows its laden branches toward the earth. Thus does nature declare and testify that Brama hath blessed her with riches. But thou art like a rock, the spring of which is dried up. If these words do not convince thee, Dushmanta, ask the tears of thy people, and then pride thyself upon thy wealth, before the face of Brama, and of the universe which he hath created."

Thus spake the hermit, and he returned to his cottage. But Dushmanta took the words of the Bramin to heart, and he again became a benefactor and a blessing to his people.

After this he repaired one day to the cottage of the Bramin, and called him forth, and said—"I may now venture to appear once more in the rays of the bounteous sun, and in the presence of thy tree, laden with its fruit. But one thing is still wanting."

"And what," asked the Bramin, "can be wanting to that prince, who is a blessing to his country, and a father to his people?"

"I have still," answered Dushmanta, "to offer the grateful tribute of my heart to that wisdom which has led me into the right path, and taught me that the glad looks of a people are the sole riches of their prince and ruler. I had become poor; thou hast made me once more inexpressibly rich."

Thus spake the prince, and the venerable man embraced him with tears of joy, and blessed him.

## THE GYPSIES.

THE LOST CHILD AND THE GYPSIES.

GYPSIES are a class of people, who have no settled place to live in, but wander about from spot to spot, and sleep at night in tents, or in barns. We have no gypsies in our country, for here every person can find employment of some kind, and there is no excuse for idlers and vagrants. But in many parts of Europe, the gypsies are very numerous; and they are often wicked and troublesome. It is said that they are descendants of the Egyptians, and have lived a wandering life ever since the year

1517, at which time they refused to submit to the Turks, who were the conquerors of Egypt.

Being banished from their native country, the gypsies agreed to unite in small parties, and to disperse themselves over different parts of the earth. There are not so many of them now as there used to be, but they are still to be found in considerable numbers, in Spain, Germany and many other parts of Europe.

Well; I have a short story to tell you about these gypsies. Many years ago as the boat which carries passengers from Leyden to Amsterdam, was putting off, a boy run along the side of the canal, and desired to be taken in. The master of the boat, however, refused to take him, because he had not quite money enough to pay the usual fare.

A rich merchant being pleased with the looks of the boy, whom I shall call Albert, and being touched with compassion towards him, paid the money for him, and ordered him to be taken on board. The little fellow thanked the merchant for his kindness and jumped into the boat. Upon talking with him afterwards, the merchant found that Albert could speak readily in three or four different languages. He also learned that the boy had been stolen away when a child by a gypsy, and had rambled ever since, with a gang of these strollers, up and down several parts of Europe.

It happened, that the merchant, whose heart

seems to have inclined towards the boy by a secret kind of instinct, had himself lost a child some years before. The parents, after a long search for him, had concluded that he had been drowned in one of the canals, with which the country abounds; and the mother was so afflicted at the loss of her son, that she died for grief of him.

Upon comparing all particulars, and examining the marks, by which the child was described when he was first missing, Albert proved to be the long lost son of the merchant. The lad was well pleased to find a father who was so kind and generous; while the father was not a little delighted to see a son return to him, whom he had given up for lost.

Albert possessed a quick understanding, and could speak with fluency several different languages. In time he rose to eminence and was much respected for his talents and knowledge. He is said to have visited, as a public minister, several countries in which he formerly wandered as a gypsy.

## LITTLE FOUR-TOES.

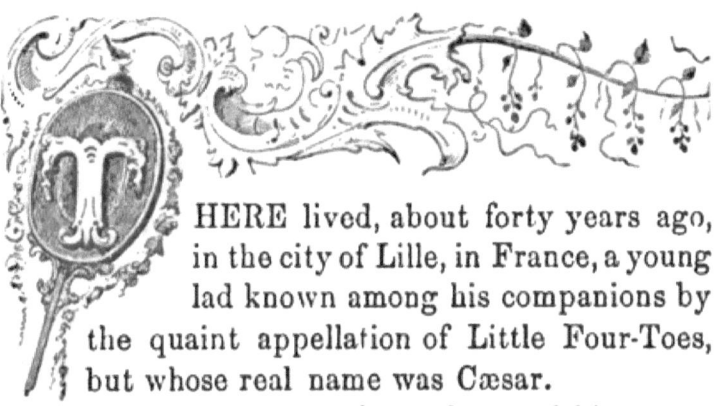

THERE lived, about forty years ago, in the city of Lille, in France, a young lad known among his companions by the quaint appellation of Little Four-Toes, but whose real name was Cæsar.

His father was a poor shoemaker, and his greatest exertions were barely adequate to supply himself and family with the common necessaries of life.

Cæsar had the misfortune to be born without hands or arms, the upper part of his legs, by a strange freak of nature, had been left out of his organization, and each foot was supplied with only four toes.

Under this accumulation of poverty and misfortune, he seemed destined to live a life of want and misery; but his fate happily proved otherwise.

While still young, Cæsar became quite dexterous with his feet, using them very expertly in the place of hands, in the common games of his playmates, and at the time our sketch opens, he was the best penman in Mr. Dumoncelle's writing school, which proves that hands are not at all necessary to the welfare of a genius, however needful they may be to ordinary mortals.

One morning as Cæsar entered the little school-room of M. Dumoncelle, he observed the master seated at his desk, turning over the leaves of his (Cæsar's) copy-book with rather an impatient hand.

"How is this, Cæsar," said the master, sternly, as he eyed the blushing boy; "how is this, that you, usually so diligent, have of late wasted your time and disfigured your copy-book with these fantastic figures? This is not the way to prepare yourself for becoming a good writing-teacher!"

"Ah! master," replied the boy, "I hope you will not be angry with me; but I have given up that idea. I do not wish to become a writing-teacher."

"What then, pray?"

"A painter!"

"A painter!" said the master, in surprise; "when did you get that foolish notion into your head? I thought you had fully determined to earn a living by teaching penmanship."

"And so I had," Cæsar replied; "but when I looked upon those beautiful paintings in Watley's Picture Gallery, my soul seemed stirred with nobler impulses, and I determined, whatever trials and hardships it might cost me to be a painter—nothing but a painter."

"Ah! but, Cæsar, you must not forget your natural deformities, which unsuit you for following painting as a profession, and that it will take a great deal of money to support you while preparing for an artist's career. As a teacher of penmanship, you can succeed—as a painter, never."

"How do you know that, friend Dumoncelle?" said a gentleman, as he advanced from the doorway into the room. "You are a good writing-master, but you are no judge of painting or painters. Better leave that business to me."

"Gladly will I, M. Watley; so, if you please, look over these pen-and-ink sketches, and give this boy your opinion of them," replied the master, as he handed Cæsar's copy-book to the gentleman.

In the mean time, Cæsar stood near by, with downcast eyes and flushed face, fully expecting a severe reprimand from M. Watley, who was a noted painter, and at that time President of the School of Design in Lille.

But as the critic said nothing, Cæsar gathered courage and looked up.

Watley was turning over the leaves of the copy-book slowly, but was evidently pleased.

When he reached the last picture, he said, "These are excellently done, my lad, for one so young. Give me your hand; I welcome you into the brotherhood of artists."

But Cæsar smiled sadly, as he said, "Ah! monsieur, I am without hands."

"Without hands!" repeated Watley, in surprise, for he had not before noticed this misfortune of Cæsar. "How, then, pray, did you make these pictures?"

"With my feet," replied the lad, modestly.

"The boy is a prodigy, a genius," murmured the astonished painter. "You shall be a painter, my lad," he continued, "if you wish it. I myself will get you admitted into the School of Design."

Cæsar was overjoyed at a prospect of a fulfillment of his long-cherished hopes, and, hardly waiting to thank M. Watley for his generous offer, he hurried home to tell his parents of the proposal of the artist.

A few days after this, Cæsar was admitted into the School of Design, and from that time his course was steadily upward.

After a few years of hard study, and steady application, he received from the hands of his generous patron, M. Watley, the highest prize for painting; and deeming rightly that, to be a good painter he must put himself under the tuition of better artists than his native city afforded, he removed to Paris.

Here, in a few years, his reputation was established, and he became the successful and admired painter, Cæsar Ducornet, for by this name was Little Four-Toes known throughout the world.

You may be sure, however famous and honored

he was, that he did not forget, in his prosperity, his poor parents. As soon as possible, they were sent for to come to his residence in Paris ; and he whom one might suppose an object of charity, generously supported them until his death, which occurred in 1856.

May this short story of his life nerve some youthful spirit in the struggle against adverse circumstances, and aid it to bear with patient courage the burden which misfortune has entailed upon it.

## THE ELVES OF THE FOREST CENTRE.

THERE lived a little girl, named Maia, with her mother, in a deep forest. As they had always dwelt in the same lone spot, the child had become accustomed to the solitude of the surrounding woods, and even loved the old trees that towered above her head.

So she was not surprised when, one bright morning, her mother said : " Maia, take thy little basket, and go to the forest centre, and fetch a few fagots and some nuts."

Maia quickly put on her gipsy hat, bade her mother good-bye, and tripped away. She knew all the little birds and squirrels ; she did not fear even the king of beasts, so gentle was he to her. And oh ! when the young tigers leaped forth to meet her, she could not help setting her basket down, to take a nice tumble upon the soft moss. Then the old tiger and tigress came home, bringing four little lions to spend the day. So they carried Maia on their backs by turn, until they reached the forest centre, then, wagging their tails, they left her, all alone.

Hark ! a rustling among the dry branches—only the wind, or a squirrel in its nest—Maia began to fill her basket from a store of nuts, hidden in a hollow stump, and to tie up her fagots, for she must

DANCE OF THE FAIRIES.

hasten; but soon she dropped her basket, the fagots were forgotten, for there, before her, were the little Elves of the forest; yes, the dear, funny little Elves, whose history her mother had so often told her.

A little Elfin stole to her side, to see what she might be, and Maia was half tempted to seize the tiny creature, but something bade her not, so she only said: "Oh, how beautiful thou art!" At this the little Elf darted away, but soon returned to say: "Our king desires thee to come and feast with us, oh! great giantess!"

Maia, quite bewildered, followed the little maid, and soon found herself in the presence of the Elfin king, a tiny fellow, about as tall as her hand, and dressed in a robe of crimson velvet, spangled with diamonds. As she began to blush and courtesy, he said: "Maia, thou art a good child; we have watched thee, day by day; all the beasts of the forest love thee. They say, 'So kind and gentle is little Maia that we would not harm her.' We, too, love, and will befriend thee."

He paused, and a little Elf came forth to dance. When the dance was finished, Maia sang a song about the Elves, which pleased the king very much; then all sat down to the banquet, which was composed of the most delicate food ever known. When all were done feasting, the Elves sang another song, after which Maia was again called by the king:

"Here," he said, leading forward the Elfin maid whom she had before met, "here is a little one for thee; **guard** her well, and she will be a faithful friend."

"**How can** I repay thy kindness?" cried **Maia**; **but** before she could say more, she found herself in a beautiful little carriage, drawn by twelve rob**ins, and at** her **side sat the** maiden Elfletta, given **her by the king.** Soon **she arrived at home,** where she had **long** been expected; but **where** was the **basket** of nuts? where the fagots? Elfletta soon answered that question, by pointing to another **Elf, who was** seen in the distance, bringing them, **and** many other nice things.

**But this good fortune** did not make Maia forget her duties, **and I am sure she set** a good example **for** Elfletta, **by** rising early, **and** cheerfully performing her labors. At the **forest** centre, the Elves were always glad to see her, and the tigers always glad to carry her there.

When she grew older, the little Elfin maid **found a little** Elfin man, and, as they loved **each** other, they were married. Then Maia's good old mother died, blessing the dear daughter who had been a comfort to her in all her trials. And when Maia found gray hairs among her own dark tresses—when her hand failed, and she grew old and feeble, there had sprung up around her a little family of Elves—then did they befriend her, and she loved **them more than ever.**

Her eyes grew dim, she lay down to rest, and with her last breath blessed the little Elves. Upon the bed lay a cold form, with a calm smile upon the face; the heart did not beat, the eyes were fixed, the old woman was at rest, but was she there? No; in the sky were a host of angels—they bore the soul of *Maia* to its heavenly home.

## ADVENTURES OF CATLIN.

AN interesting letter has lately been written by a young man in Brazil, in which he relates in a very amusing manner, some of his adventures while traveling with Catlin, the famous traveler and explorer. They proceeded together some 1500 miles by land and by water, through forests and swamps and prairies, following the course ot the Amazon. It should be stated that Catlin was known in the party by the name of "Governor." The first anecdote relates

How the Old Chief was Astonished by a Colt. —"The Governor had one of Colt's pistols in his belt, and one of his revolving rifles always in his hand, and I had the old Minie, with whose power you are somewhat acquainted. I had let out the idea that the Governor's gun could shoot all day without reloading, which made an illustration necessary.—They were all anxious to see it 'set in motion,' and I placed the door of our tent, which was part of a cow skin stretched on a hoop, at the distance of sixty or seventy yards, with a bull's eye in the centre. The whole village had assembled, and the Governor took his position and went off, one! two! three! four! five! six! I then stepped up and told him that was enough, I presumed; and while the old Chief was assuring him that they were all convinced, and it was a pity to waste any more ammunition, the Governor was slipping the empty cylinder off and another one on, with six charges more, without their observing what he was doing. He offered to proceed, but all were satisfied that his gun would shoot all day without stopping, and this report traveled ahead of us to all the tribes we afterwards visited in that region."

The next is a Tiger story:

KEEP COOL AND DON'T SPILL THE GRAVY.—" One day, when we had landed, and most of our party were lying asleep on the boat, which was drawn under the shade of some large trees, the Governor and I had collected wood and made a large fire, over which we were roasting a fat pig which I had shot from the boat during the morning. I was squat down on one side of the fire, holding a short handled frying-pan, in which we had made some very rich gravy, which the Governor, who was squatted down opposite to me, was ladling over the pig, with an Indian wooden spoon. All of a sudden, I observed his eye fixed upon something over my shoulder, when he said to me in a very low tone, 'Now I want you to keep perfectly cool, and don't spill your gravy—there is a splendid tiger behind you!' I held fast to the frying-pan, and turning my head gradually around, I had a full view of the fellow within eight paces of me, lying flat on his side, and with his paws lifting up and playing with the legs of one of the Spaniards, who had laid himself down upon his belly and was fast asleep. Our rifles were left in the boat! The Governor drew himself gradually down the bank, on his hands and feet, ordering me not to move; I was in hopes he would have taken my old Minie, but he preferred his own weapon, and getting it to bear upon the beast, he was obliged to wait some minutes for it to raise its head, so as not to endanger the poor Spaniard; at the crack of the rifle the animal gave a piercing screech, and leaped about 15 feet straight in the air, and fell quite dead. The Spaniard leaped nearly as far in a different direction; and at the same instant, from behind a little bunch of bushes on the opposite side, and not half the distance from our fire, and right behind the Governor's back, where he had been sitting, sprang the mate, which darted into the thicket and disappeared. We skinned this beautiful animal, which was shot exactly between the eyes, and after all hands had withdrawn to the boat, waited several hours in hopes that the other one would show itself again, but we waited in vain, and lost our game."

## THE PANTHER HUNT.

THREE powerful, slenderly-formed hounds were coursing along through the dense forest, with their noses close to the ground, sometimes leaving the track amid the dry leaves, and snuffing about the fallen trees, and old, half-decayed trunks, then renewing the chase with loud baying—a certain sign that they were in pursuit of a wild beast, either a bear or a panther, and not the swift-footed deer, which, when it crossed their path, enticed them for a short time only from their track, but never entirely put them on a false scent.

They had now reached a spot, where the object of their chase had evidently delayed for a while, and must have crossed their path, for they often stopped for a moment, and then springing with wild yells back and forth, sought with increased eagerness around some closely-entwined plants, which encircled the spot, forming an almost impassable barrier, but again returned to its centre, there to renew their howls and lamentations.

Suddenly the bushes were pushed aside, and a young man mounted upon a small, black Indian pony, with a broad hunting knife in his hand, which he made use of to cut through the hanging vines, that threatened to drag him from his horse, appeared among the hounds, which, at his sudden appearance, surrounded him for a moment, barking and wagging their tails, and then, incited by the presence of their master, renewed their search with increased eagerness.

"Right, my good dogs!" cried the young man, checking his horse, while he thrust his knife into its sheath, and placed the long rifle which he carried upon his shoulder, upon the saddle-bow before him, "that's right! seek, seek—you are upon the

THE HOUND.

track, and I think we shall this time catch the thief that has stolen so many of our young pigs—he has escaped us often enough."

"Hip! hip!" he cried, raising himself high in his stirrups, and shouting his hunting cry, as he saw that the oldest of the dogs had suddenly found the track again, and, followed by the others, at once disappeared in the thicket—" hip! hip!" and throwing his rifle again upon his shoulder, he grasped the reins with his right hand, plunging his spurs into his horse's flanks, which reared aloft, and then dashed wildly after the hounds.

Nothing slackened their eagerness; neither the fallen trees, the dense thicket, marshes, nor miry channels; onward they coursed, and the horse, snorting and foaming, followed them with his master, who uttered loud, cheering huzzas.

The hounds now paused anew; this time, however, it was not uncertainty concerning the direction their enemy had taken that restrained their pursuit, for they leaped up, barking and yelling, against a lofty oak, furiously biting the roots and the rough bark of the mighty tree that gave shelter to the foe, and protected him from his pursuers.

The hunter now appeared on the scene of action, and without waiting for his horse to pause in his career, sprang with a bound from the saddle, leaving the riderless beast to his own will. He then walked slowly about the tree, peering inquisitively through the dense foliage, and at last saw, ensconced between two branches, the form of a living creature, which, nestling closely to one of them, probably thought itself concealed and unobserved.

It was indeed quite dark in the shadow of the thick leaves, and a less practiced eye than that of our young forester must have long remained in doubt as to the name and species of the beast that seemed so carefully intent upon withdrawing itself from the view of the hunter below. Wilson's keen glance, however, soon recognized in the cowering form a panther's cub, that was easily betrayed by its long tail, which it was unable to conceal.

He had already raised his rifle, to dislodge the animal from its height, where it doubtless thought itself secure, while the hounds gazed, breathless and expectant, now at the barrel of the rifle, from which they every moment expected to see flame flash forth, now at the top of the tree, in which they knew that their enemy was concealed.

But their low, imploring whine, with which they thought to hasten their master's shot, was this time in vain; the latter appeared suddenly to have changed his mind; he lowered his rifle, and again began to examine the tree with even greater attention than before.

After a long and careful investigation, he seemed at last to have satisfied himself with regard to what he wished to know; he leaned his rifle against a fallen trunk that lay not far from the tree, unbuckled his belt, in which were thrust a knife and a small tomahawk, drew off his hunting shirt, and then, holding his belt in his hand, returned to the oak, which the hounds, although they had followed attentively every movement of their master, had not quitted for an instant.

"I will try it!" he muttered at last to himself. "I will try and take him alive; if I carry him to Little Rock, I can, with ease, get ten or fifteen dollars for him; if I shoot him, his hide isn't worth much. Besides, the mother must have fled, for I can't see her anywhere in the tree, and for ten dollars a man may very well take a scratching once from such a young chap; so then, my little panther, look out, for I am coming!"

With these words he walked to his horse, which was grazing quietly, unwound a rope that was fastened about his neck, buckled his belt about him again, in which he replaced his knife, leaving his tomahawk and rifle behind him, and began to ascend the huge tree. This he accomplished in the following manner: casting the rope high about the body of the tree, where a knob prevented it from slipping, he seized it by the two ends, and raised himself carefully, now with the right arm, now with the left, until he reached a part of the trunk which was sufficiently slender for him to grasp it firmly in his arms. The hounds at once comprehended their master's intention, and sprang, barking and yelping around the roots of the oak.

Slowly and cautiously the hunter climbed the tree to a height of about forty feet, before he reached the lower limb, where he could take breath and rest for a moment. When here, he felt for his knife to see that it was in its place, glancing up at the young panther, which still lay nestling close to the same branch upon which he had first observed it, wound the rope, which he no longer needed for his ascent, about his shoulders, and using the branches as the steps of a natural ladder, ascended rapidly and lightly towards the panther, which lay without stirring indeed, but kept its gloomy eyes fixed upon the approaching enemy.

But other and more ferocious glances observed and watched the progress of the hunter, who had not the slightest presentiment of this new and dangerous neighbor. It was no other than the cub's mother, which, crouching upon the limb of an adjacent tree, the branches of which projected among those of the oak, lay ready to leap, and waving her tail slowly, seemed only to be waiting for the hunter's nearer approach to spring upon the bold aggressor, who ventured to attack her offspring.

Wilson swung himself carelessly from branch to branch, and was already close beneath the young panther, which now rose softly, and raising its back after the fashion of a cat, stood upon the branch, and looked down at the hunter, as if not yet quite understanding the danger which his presence betokened.

Wilson now paused, unwound the rope from his shoulders, made a noose at one end of it, cast it over the cub's head, and supporting himself upon two other branches, was in the act of looking up, to avail himself of the proper moment, when he beheld directly opposite to him, at a distance of scarcely ten paces, the glowing eyes of the mother, who, at this instant, was crouching to make a spring.

Reared from childhood in the forest, and familiar with the dangers which so often menace the solitary hunter, he retained in that fearful moment sufficient presence of mind to bring the trunk of the oak instantly, and before his enemy could divine his intention, between him and the beast, which he succeeded in doing by a rapid movement. But it was indeed high time, for at that very moment, the dark form of the panther sprang to the spot which he had just abandoned, and her glowing eyes gazed into those of the undaunted hunter, who, with his left arm wound about a branch, and holding in his right hand a drawn knife, expected every instant to see the infuriated animal leap down upon him.

The panther, however, intimidated by the glance which the hunter kept fixed upon her, seemed satisfied with knowing that her cub was protected, and with carefully watching every movement of her enemy, and kept her present position, which was scarcely six feet distant from him.

At first Wilson gave himself up for lost, for although his knife was a good, strong weapon, even against the most dangerous animal, yet the place where he stood, and where the slightest misstep would have hurled him lifeless to the ground, was by no means well calculated for a combat with such an enemy. No sooner, therefore, did he find that his antagonist contented herself with watching him merely, than he rapidly, but carefully, and without any hurried movement which could have alarmed or enraged the monster, restored his knife to its sheath, and slowly commenced to descend the tree.

The panther seeing that he retired farther and farther from her, followed him slowly, and more than once Wilson's hand grasped after his weapon, when he observed the beast's slender form couched to spring; still, however, the latter could not resolve to venture an open attack, eye to eye.

Thus he reached the lowermost branch, again wound the rope about the trunk, grasped its two ends, and slid carefully, but as rapidly as possible to the ground.

The hounds, in the mean while, had observed their enemy as it had followed their master, and driven to wild fury, at seeing the beast among the branches without being able to reach her, they leaped aloft, and barked and yelled most piteously.

At last Wilson had gained firm ground again; his garments were torn, the blood dropped from his arms, which had been severely lacerated by the rough bark of the oak, his strength was exhausted, and his knees shook beneath him. Not an instant, however, did he allow himself for repose; he sprang towards the spot where he had left his rifle, grasped it, and raised it to his cheek, to bring the panther from the retreat which it thought so secure. But it was in vain that he endeavored to hold the heavy weapon still and motionless even for a second; his limbs trembled, and he was obliged to cast himself upon the ground to obtain a moment's repose. But not an eye did he turn from the beast, that now cowered closely to the trunk, near its cub, which fearing no more danger, stood upon a somewhat projecting branch, with lifted tail, and rubbed itself comfortably against its mother.

Wilson soon recovered himself, grasped his rifle once more, took a long and sure aim, and the echo of his weapon resounded, thundering, from the distant hills.

The beast, pierced by the fatal bullet, started convulsively, sprang aloft, clambered in wild haste from limb to limb, to the top of the tree; the thin branches yielded beneath her; she had now nearly reached the summit of the oak when the weak foliage gave way; she fell, yet in falling, her powerful claws still grasped at the leaves and tendrils, until at last, with a mighty crash, amid the loud howlings of the dogs, she dropped lifeless at Wilson's feet.

No farther obstacle now stood in the way of his taking the cub alive, which had anxiously followed its mother to the lowermost branches of the tree, yet his first experiment had too severely exhausted his strength, and he was unable again to attempt the laborious task. He therefore reloaded his rifle, and a sure shot brought the cub within the reach of the hounds, which assailed it with great fury.

In a few moments, the hides of the two panthers were stripped off, and placed upon the pony, and followed by the hounds, the bold hunter rode to new booty and to new dangers.

THE MAMMOTH CAVE.

## THE MAMMOTH CAVE.

ONE of the most remarkable caves in the world, if not the most remarkable yet discovered, is found in Kentucky. From its immense and yet unknown extent, it is generally called "The Mammoth Cave." Its entrance is a little south of Green River, in Edmonson County, and some half dozen miles east from Browneville, the capital of that county. Being nearly midway between Louisville and Frankfort on the north, and Nashville on the south, it has become quite a fashionable resort from those places, as well as for the multitude of travelers from all sections, who annually go forth in quest of wonders. Ample accommodation for all such is provided by the forecast of Dr. Crogan, who purchased, a few years ago, a large tract of land in the vicinity, and erected, near the entrance, an extensive hotel, which he called "The Cave House." The main building is a spacious airy frame, two hundred feet long and two stories high, substantially built of logs, neatly finished on the outside with clap-boards, and made picturesque and comfortable by green blinds, porticoes, verandahs, etc. This building is flanked, at either end, by substantial wings of brick, which show their gable ends in front, making the whole facade about three hundred feet in length.

The approach to the cave as delineated in the accompanying engraving, is beautiful and romantic, though the country, for some distance round, is one of those dry, unpromising tracts of rolling knobs and hills, which sometimes occur in the prairie country, on which it seems that nothing can grow but dwarf oaks, or beeches, or such vines and shrubs as can find a precarious rooting in the hard baked soil. The immediate neighborhood of the Cave House is more agreeable and inviting—sufficiently so to redeem in part the general character of the section. Patches of thrifty woodland, elm, hickory, chestnut, and other species of valuable and ornamental trees, in which there are fine openings, and romantic reaches for pleasant walks and rides, with sharp ravines widening into delightful valleys, present some landscapes of rare beauty.

Cave Hollow is a deep valley bounded by walls of lime-rock, overlaid with sandstone. In some places the sides are precipitous and sharp; in others, composed of loose, broken masses of rock piled rudely together, and overgrown with a wild luxuriance of clambering vines, brambles, and flowers of various hues, while the valley below is thickly set with maples, walnuts, catalpas, paw-paws, etc.

A circuitous path through this hollow, leads to the entrance of the Cave. This is a dark, gloomy-looking opening in the side of the hill, some fifteen feet high, and perhaps twenty feet broad at the base.

It does not appear, in passing, as large as this, and, indeed, might well be passed by without notice, being liberally overhung with vines and shrubbery. From this entrance there is a descent of thirty feet, or more, over somewhat broken and irregular stone steps, to the first floor or level, to which you enter through an archway of loosly piled rocks, overgrown with a tangled vegetation, through which there is a constant dripping of water from above. The outward current of cold air which meets you at the first entrance becomes here more intensely cold, and much stronger, so that you must look well to your torches.

The vestibule of the Cave is a hall of an oval shape, two hundred feet in length by one hundred and fifty wide, with a *roof as flat and level as if finished by the trowel*, and from fifty to sixty feet high. Two passages, each a hundred feet in width, open into it at the opposite extremities, but at right angles to each other; and as they run in a straight course for five or six hundred feet, with the same flat roof common to each, the appearance presented to the eye is that of a vast hall in the shape of the letter L., expanded at the angle, both branches being *five hundred feet long by one hundred wide.* The entire extent of this prodigious space is *covered by a single rock, in which the eye can detect no break or interruption*, save at its borders, which are surrounded by a broad sweeping cornice, traced in horizontal panel work, exceedingly noble and regular. *Not a single pier or pillar of any kind contributes to support it.* It needs no support, but is

'By its own weight made steadfast and immovable.'

Lee describes "The Temple" as "an immense vault, covering an erea of two acres, and covered by a single dome of solid rock, one hundred and twenty feet high. It excels in size the cave of Staffa, and rivals the celebrated vault in the Grotto of Antiparos, which is said to be the largest in the world. In passing through from one end to the other, the dome appears to follow, like the sky in passing from place to place on the earth. In the middle of the dome there is a large mound of rocks, rising on one side nearly to the top, very steep, and forming what is called the *mountain*. When first I ascended this mound from the cave below, I was struck with a feeling of awe, more deep and intense than anything I had ever before experienced. I could only observe the narrow circle which was illuminated immediately around me ; above and beyond was apparently an unlimited space, in which the ear could not catch the slightest sound, nor the eye find an object to rest upon. It was filled with silence and darkness; and yet I knew that I was beneath the earth, and that this space, however large it might be, was actually bounded by solid walls. My curiosity was rather excited than gratified. In order that I might see the whole in one connected view, I built fires in many places, with the pieces of cane which I found scattered among the rocks. Then taking my stand on the mountain a scene was presented of surprising magnificence. On the opposite side, the strata of gray limestone, breaking up by steps from the bottom, could scarcely be discerned in the distance by the glimmering. Above was the lofty dome, closed at the top by a smooth slab beautifully defined in the outline, from which the walls sloped away on the right and left into thick darkness. Every one has heard of the dome of the mosque of St. Sophia, of St. Peter's, and St. Paul's; they are never spoken of but in terms of admiration, as the chief works of architecture, and among the noblest, and most stupendous examples of what man can do when aided by science; and yet, when compared with the dome of this temple, they sink into comparative insignificance. Such is the surpassing grandeur of nature's works."

## THE PUMP.

IN France and Germany you will find that one of the social institutions most popular with the masses, is the town pump or fountain, where, at early dawn, and at nightfall, the assembled servants from all the neighborhood, with their pails or pitchers in hand, hold their levee. You will see them standing in little groups around, in earnest conversation with each other ; their cheerful faces and animated gestures indicating that they are in no unhappy mood. These pumps or fountains, as the case may be, are often very elaborate in their workmanship, and really ornamental to the street or square where they are located. The fountains that abound in the squares in Paris, with their broad basins and elegant statuary, are among the finest ornaments of the city.

In some of the provincial towns these fountains have become the more interesting from their great antiquity, and from the historic associations connected with them. Here you will find an immense stone basin, which, perhaps ten centuries ago, was, as now, the rendezvous for water-bearers, and there the huge stone pump whose dog-head spout has for ages supplied the limpid beverage. If they could speak and tell what they have heard and seen, what changes have been wrought while they have stood unchanged; if they could repeat the gossip and love-tales of other days, how they would enchain the attentive listeners!

THE PUMP.

While we admired these pumps and fountains for their artistic interest, and some for their antiquity, we were more attracted by their social position. They every day witness many a merry group and greeting, while they often hear gossip that were better not repeated. They hear, too, the thousand little narratives, and discussions, and sallies of wit and repartee that give the zest to social life, and make society a blessing. Long may they stand in their social position to witness the joyous greetings of a happy people.

## A BANKER IN TROUBLE.

HERE is a story of a rich foreigner, named Sutherland, naturalized in Russia, who was banker to the Court, and in high favor with the Empress. He was roused one morning by the information that his house was surrounded by guards, and that Reliew, the Minister of Police, desired to speak with him. This personage entering without further ceremony, at once announced his errand.

"Mr. Sutherland," said he, "I am charged by my gracious sovereign with the execution of a sentence, the severity of which both astonishes and grieves me ; and I am ignorant as to how you can so far have excited the resentment of her majesty."

"I am as much in the dark as yourself," replied the banker ; "but what are your orders ?"

"I have not the courage to tell you."

"Have I lost the confidence of the Empress ?"

"If that were all, you would not see me troubled —confidence may return—position may be restored."

"Am I to be sent back to my own country? or good heavens!" cried the banker trembling, "does the Empress think of banishing me to Siberia?"

"Alas! you might some day return."

"Am I to be knouted?"

"This punishment is fearful, but—it does not kill!"

"Is my *life*, then, in peril? I can not believe that the Empress, usually so mild and gentle—who spoke to me so kindly but two days since—'tis impossible!—for Heaven's sake let me know the worst; anything is better than this intolerable suspense."

"Well, then," said Reliew, in a melancholy tone, "my gracious mistress has ordered me to have you *stuffed*."

"*Stuffed?*" cried the poor banker, horrified.

"Yes, stuffed with straw."

Sutherland looked fixedly at the Minister of Police an instant, and exclaimed:

"Sir, either you have lost your reason, or the Empress is not in her right senses; surely you did not receive such a command without endeavoring, at least, to point out its unreasonableness, its barbarity."

"Alas, my unfortunate friend, I did that which, under ordinary circumstances, I should not have dared to attempt; I manifested my grief, my consternation, I even hazarded an humble remonstrance; but her imperial majesty, in an irritated tone, bade me leave her presence, and see her commands obeyed *at once;* adding these words, which are still ringing in my ears: 'Go, and forget not that it is your duty to acquit yourself without a murmur, of any commission with which I may deign to trust you.'"

It would be impossible to describe the horror, the despair of the unhappy banker; after waiting till the first burst of grief was over, Reliew informed him that he would be allowed a quarter of an hour to settle his worldly affairs. Sutherland wept, and prayed, and entreated the minister to take a petition from him to the Empress. Overcome by his supplications the magistrate consented to be his messenger, and took charge of the missive, but afraid to return to the palace, he hastily presented himself at the residence of Earl Bruce, the English Ambassador, and explained the affair to him. The ambassador, very naturally, supposed the Minister of Police had become insane, but bidding him follow, he hurried to the palace. Introduced into the imperial presence, he told his story with as little delay as possible. On hearing this strange recital, Catherine exclaimed—

"Merciful Heaven! what a dreadful mistake! Reliew must have lost his wits—run quickly, my lord; I beg and desire that madman to relieve my poor banker of his groundless fears, and to set him at liberty immediately."

The Earl left the room to do as her majesty requested, and on his return found Catherine laughing immoderately.

"I see now," said she, "the cause of this inconceivably absurd blunder. I had, for some years, a little dog, to which I was much attached. I called him Sutherland, because that was the name of the English gentleman who presented him to me; this dog has just died, and I gave Reliew orders to have him stuffed; as he hesitated, I became angry, supposing that, from a foolish excess of pride, he thought this commission beneath his dignity. That is the solution of this ridiculous enigma."

## RUINS OF ST. BARTOLPH AT COLCHESTER.

THE distinguishing feature of the parish of St. Bartolph, in Colchester, is the ruins of its ancient priory and monastic church. These ruins have long afforded a favorite subject for the painter, while they have interested alike the lovers of antiquity and picturesque effect. Of the priory itself very little now remains, but in the view which we here present of the ruins of the church, you get some general idea of the noble and magnificent structure. A considerable portion of the building on the rear has been entirely demolished to the foundations. The length of the building that is now standing is one hundred and eight feet, the diameter of the pillars is five and a half feet, and the thickness of the wall is eight and a half feet. It is built apparently of Roman brick, which adds to the interest of the ruin. The front, which you see standing, faces westward, and is ornamented, immediately above the principal entrance, with two distinct rows of semicircular arches, which form pointed arches at their intersection, in the manner supposed to have first suggested the Gothic arch. Above these appears to have been a circular window, but how the summit of this front terminated must be a matter of conjecture, as no record reveals its form or appearance. But it is known that at

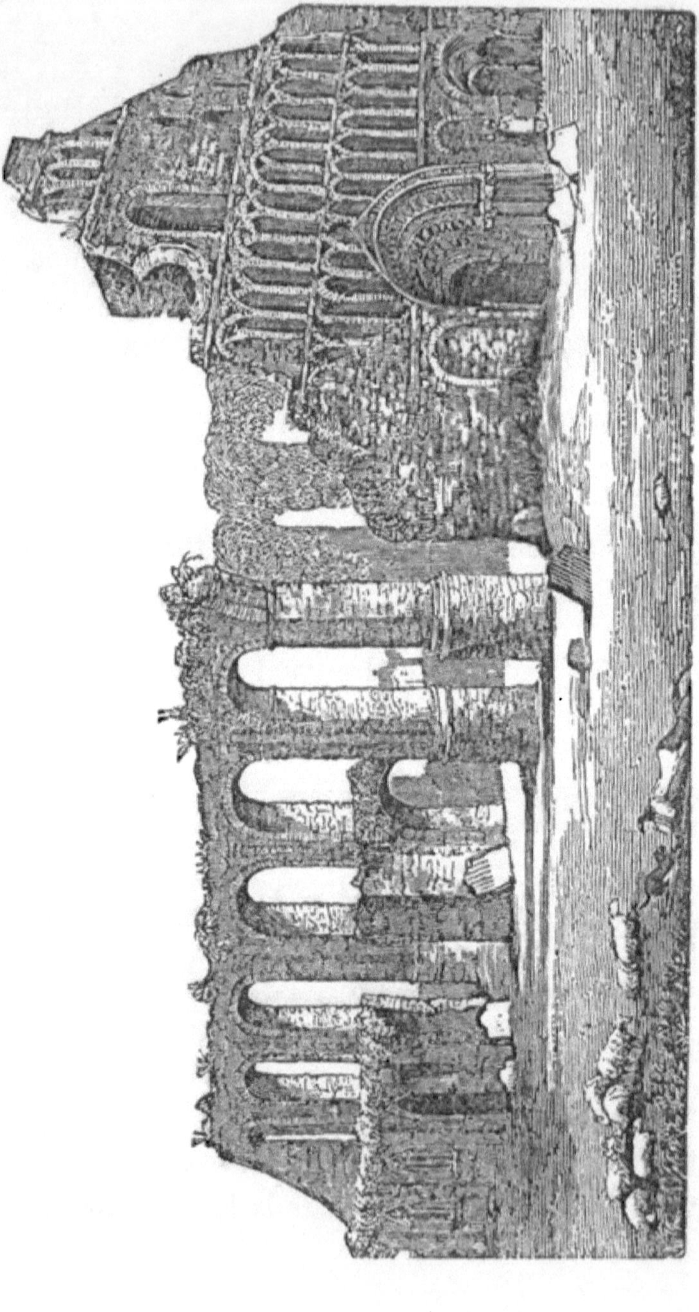

RUINS AT ST. BARTOLPH AT COLCHESTER.

either angle of the front there was a stately tower, of which "the northwest was standing," says Morant, "within the memory of man."

The front entrance is by a deeply receding semicircular arch, and is one of the best specimens extant of the grand Norman doorway. Much of this entrance is hidden from the spectator by the accumulation of earth about it to a considerable height, yet from the representation, as it now appears in the cut, it is evident that it was a magnificent affair.

The prevalence of the pure Roman arch, unaccompanied by Gothic ornaments, in these remains, points to a period for the origin of this structure when the Normans had only began to conceive of the *pointed* order of architecture. If you examine the cut closely, you will observe that some of the arches are circular, and others are pointed or Gothic; for instance, the arches of the windows in the north aisle are evidently pointed, and from that circumstance it is naturally inferred that that portion of the structure is of later origin.

The origin of this monastic establishment is involved in some obscurity, but it was founded about the beginning of the twelfth century. At the time of the dissolution of monasteries in England, this priory, including its lands, and buildings, and revenues, was valued at more than half a million of dollars, and was given by Henry VIII. to Sir Thomas

Audley, then Lord Chancellor of England—it has since passed through various hands. The walls of the priory are entirely demolished, and a brewery is now erected on the site. We hope the ruin of the church will long be spared from a like fate, for, aside from its picturesque effect, it must always be viewed with interest by the traveler as a connecting link between the present and the past, and as such is more eloquent than pen or tongue. There is not a pillar, or arch, or stone, from the foundation to the summit, that does not speak impressively to the beholder. Say what we will, there is a wonderful power in architecture to move our minds to sublime emotions, and when to its other qualities it adds the venerable attractions of age and decay, the emotion which we feel is closely allied to a spirit of devotion.

## MY HEART'S IN THE HIGHLANDS.

HUNTING the deer is the favorite sport of the Highlanders. Full of the love of adventure, they enter into the chase with all the enthusiasm of their mountain nature, and amid all the perils and dangers to which they are liable, and in whatever land their lot is cast, their heart is still for the Highlands, and they sing their old familiar song, and long to go back to the thrilling scenes and wonderful adventures of their mountain home.

### THE HIGHLANDER'S SONG.

My heart's in the Highlands, my heart is not here;
My heart's in the Highlands a-chasing the deer:
A-chasing the wild deer, and following the roe,
My heart's in the Highlands wherever I go.
Farewell to the Highlands, farewell to the North,
The birth-place of valor, the country of worth;
Wherever I wander, wherever I rove,
The hills of the Highlands for ever I love.
Farewell to the mountains high covered with snow;
Farewell to the straths and green valleys below;
Farewell to the forests and wild-hanging woods;
Farewell to the torrents and loud-pouring floods.
My heart's in the Highlands, my heart is not here,
My heart's in the Highlands a-chasing the deer;
Chasing the wild deer, and following the roe,
My heart's in the Highlands wherever I go.

## THE PALACE OF THE ESCURIAL.

THIRTY miles to the westward of Madrid, in Spain, and upon the mountain side, in the midst of bold and striking scenery, is the famous palace of the Escurial—the largest and most expensive palace in the world. It was built by Philip II. in the latter part of the sixteenth century, in fulfillment of a vow which he made on the occasion of the battle of St. Quentin, in 1557. In that battle, in which his army fought against the French, he vowed that if he should gain a victory, he would build a monastery, a church, and a palace in honor of the occasion.

It so happened that the battle of St. Quentin was won on St. Bartholomew's day, and Philip determined also to do honor to that saint by constructing the palace in the form and after the model of a gridiron—St. Bartholomew having suffered martyrdom by broiling on a gridiron.

The fancy was congenial to the austere and gloomy mind of Philip, who seems to have delighted in thoughts and deeds of cruelty. We can readily conceive how a man like Philip, who poisoned his own son, Don Carlos, for defending the rights of the people, and who divorced his queen without reason, could have special sympathy with thoughts and images of cruelty, and could find pleasure in surrounding himself with the memorials of torture. Accordingly he not only built his palace, which was intended to be a master-piece of regal splendor, in form of a gridiron, but he simulated that instrument on all its doors and windows, and on the altar-pieces and interior ornaments.

Philip lived at a time when Spain possessed immense wealth. She controlled all the East India trade, received immense treasures of gold from South America, and was in a position to wield immense power among the nations. Nor was Philip destitute of talent and force of character and executive power, but he lacked those moral virtues so needful in a sovereign; so that his power declined, and when he died, there were few to deplore his loss or defend his memory.

The palace which he built upon the mountain side stands—a monument of his immense magnificence, his strange taste, and his gloomy character. It is a quadrangular building, 740 feet in length, by 580 feet in breadth, and is said to have cost fifty millions of dollars. Its principal front is towards the west, and the opposite side, which faces towards Madrid, has the form of the shortened handle of a gridiron ; while the legs of the gridiron are represented by the towers which you see projecting from the angles of the building.

The exterior of the Escurial is not magnificent in architecture. It has rather the austere simplicity of a convent than the elegance of a palace. It is built of hewn stone of a species of granite, which by time is changed to a dark brown color, giving the structure a very sombre appearance. Within there is more elegance, and the appearance of the most lavish expenditure in all the arrangements and ornaments. It has 80 staircases, 73 fountains, 1860 rooms, 8 organs, and 12,000 windows and doors.

It contains a large collection of pictures, some of which are by the best masters, and are very rich and valuable. Here are several fine paintings by Guido, Pellegrino, Navarette, Paul Veronese, Rubens, Titian, and Raphael. In the Escurial there is also a large and valuable library, founded by Philip II., and very much increased by his son. It is particularly valuable for its large collection of Greek and Arabic manuscripts.

You see the hills towering in the rear of the palace, and transcending it in their grandeur.

## TOMB OF EDWARD II.

THE annexed beautiful monument to the memory of Edward II. is erected in the Cathedral at Gloucester. Beneath the splended Gothic canopy he is represented as reposing in state.

Edward II., born in 1284, was the first English Prince of Wales, and succeeded to the throne of England in 1307. He had an agreeable figure and mild disposition, but was indolent and fond of pleasure. Previous to his coming to the throne and afterwards, England was engaged in wars with Scotland. In 1314 Edward assembled an immense army to check the progress of Robert Bruce, but was completely defeated at Bannockburn.

He was unfortunate in the selection of favorites, and in every way proved himself incompetent to his place. His queen, Isabella, was disloyal to the crown and untrue to her husband. Her paramour was Roger Mortimer, a young baron of Wales, who, in consort with the queen, determined upon the destruction of the weak and unhappy husband. They formed an association out of the discontented party, and conspired to seize the reins of government. They took possession of the Tower of London and other strong fortresses, executed without trial some of the councillors of state, and took the King prisoner, who on the commencement of the revolt had concealed himself in Wales. The unfortunate Edward was confined in Kenilworth Castle, and in the January following (1327) his deposi-

tion was unanimously agreed on by parliament, on the ground of incapacity and misgovernment.

He soon after resigned the crown, and was transferred to Berkley Castle; but Mortimer and the queen, not satisfied while he lived, pursued him to death. Two ruffians were despatched, who, it is said, murdered him in a way so as not to leave any external marks of violence. This occurred in Sept., 1327, in the twentieth year of his reign, and the forty-third of his age.

## CHURCH OF THE HOLY TRINITY, HULL.

THIS beautiful church was commenced in 1312, under the reign of Edward II. It is built after the cathedral fashion, and is the largest parochial edifice in England. It is 279 feet long ; the breadth of the nave is 172 feet ; the length of the chancel 100 feet.

The interior architecture of the church is in the first style of Gothic grandeur, and in its original state must have been pre-eminently beautiful. In the centre of the nave are three separate pulpits, of different size, but all similar in form and ornament; they are octagonal, and covered with rich panelling, and stand on four columns conjoined. They each have separate steps, and over the largest, which is more elaborately sculptured than the others, is a sounding board suspended from the roof by a chain. The interior of the chancel is very light and elegant. All the ceilings, and mouldings, and screens, of the interior of the church, are in heavy oak work, most elaborately carved, and representing various scripture subjects. At the east end is a beautiful window in most complicated and unusual style of architecture. A part of it is occupied by a painting of the Last Supper by Parmentier.

It is said that in the time of the rebellion, the passage to the main church was walled up with brick, but that the chancel was left open, and turned into a conventicle—or place for independent worship—and that here the Independents were accustomed to assemble and hold their meetings.

In the interior of the church there are many beautiful monuments, and other objects of artistic interest and value, among which may be mentioned a basso-relievo of Moses, and the brazen serpent on the cross, done in marble. The baptismal font is also very elaborate and beautiful. It stands on eight columns, of four cylinders each, and is carved out of stone in a most beautiful manner.

We will not attempt a description of the exterior building. The engraving will give you a general idea of it. There it stands—a massive and grand old pile, and there it has stood for more than five hundred years; its substantial buttresses, its gray old walls, its beautiful arches and chiselled cornices, speak to every successive generation of men, and tell them of the olden time.

It can never cease to be a matter of regret that the zeal of the Reformers, which dealt such blows against a corrupted church, should not have been satisfied without demolishing many of those grand old architectural piles in England and Scotland, which, if now standing entire, would be a pride and an ornament to the nation.

## THE SERPENT OF RHODES.

IN these days of snake-wonders and adventures, it may be interesting if we give the story of the Serpent of Rhodes. It dates back some five hundred years, and some allowance must of course be made for exaggeration. Yet his snakeship must have been truly a hideous monster, to defy so long the assaults of courageous knights, and carry terror and dismay through all the islands. We wonder that, in those days of credulity, they did not attempt to *charm* him with their incantations, and thus deprive him of his power. If there had been a modern Yankee there, he would have been after him with a bottle of chloroform, and put him to sleep instanter, and then, instead of tearing him to pieces with dogs, he would have caged him and showed him about the country on a speculation, like Barnum.

Here is the story :—

In the fourteenth century an amphibious animal, a sort of serpent or crocodile, caused much disorder in the island of Rhodes by its depredations, and several inhabitants fell victims to its rapacity. The retreat of this animal was in a cavern, situated near a swamp, at the foot of Mount St. Etienne, two miles from Rhodes. It often came out to seek its prey, and devoured sheep, cows, horses, and even the shepherds who watched over their flocks.

Many of the knights of St. John of Jerusalem had tried to destroy this monster; but after going out to attack it, they never returned. This induced Phelion de Villeneuve, the grand master of Malta, to forbid all knights, on pain of being deprived of their habit, from attacking it, or attempting any further an enterprise, which appeared to be above human powers.

All the knights obeyed the mandate of the grand master, except Dien Donne Gozen, who notwithstanding the prohibition, and without being deterred by the fate of his brethren, secretly formed the daring design of fighting this savage beast; bravely resolving to deliver the island from such a calamity, or perish in the attempt. Having learned that the serpent had no scales on its belly, he formed his enterprise on this information. From the description he had received of this enormous animal, he made a paste-board figure resembling it, and endeavored to imitate its terrific cries. He then trained two mastiffs to run to its cries, and to attach themselves immediately to the belly of the monster; while he, mounted on horseback, his lance in hand, and covered with his armor, feigned to give it blows in several places. The knight employed himself many months, every day, in this exercise, at the Chateau de Gozen, in Languedoc, to which he had repaired; and when he had trained the mastiffs sufficiently he hastened back to Rhodes.

Having repaired to church, and commended himself to God, he put on his armor, bid farewell to his wife and child, mounted his horse, and ordered his two servants to return directly to France, if he perished in the combat, but to come near him, if they perceived that he had killed the serpent, or been wounded by it. He then descended from the mountain of St. Etienne, and, approaching the haunt of the serpent, soon encountered it. Gozen struck it with his lance, but the scales prevented its taking effect.

He then prepared to redouble his blows, but his horse, frightened by the hisses of the serpent, refused to advance, and threw himself on his side. Gozen dismounted, and accompanied by his mastiffs, marched, sword in hand, towards this horrible beast. He struck him in various places, but the scales prevented him from penetrating them. The furious animal, by a blow of his tail, knocked down the knight, and would certainly have devoured him had not his two dogs fastened on the belly of the serpent, which they lacerated in a dreadful man-

THE KNIGHT BIDDING FAREWELL.

ner. The knight, favored by this help, rejoined his two mastiffs, and buried his sword in the body of the monster, which being mortally wounded, rushed on the knight, and would have crushed him to death by his weight, had not his servants, who witnessed the combat, come to his relief. The serpent was dead, and the knight had fainted. When he recovered, the first object which was presented to his view was the dead body of the serpent.

The death of the serpent was no sooner known in the city, than a crowd of the inhabitants came out to welcome their deliverer. The knights conducted him in triumph to the grand master, who, however, considered it a breach of discipline, unpardonable even on such an occasion; and regardless of the entreaties of the other knights and the important service that Gozen had rendered, sent him to prison. A council was assembled, who decided that he should be deprived of the habit of his order for his disobedience. This was done; but Villeneuve, repenting of his severity, soon restored to him, and loaded him with favors.

www.ingramcontent.com/pod-product-compliance
Lightning Source LLC
Chambersburg PA
CBHW031751230426
**43669CB00007B/579**